The rights of Nigel L. Job and L
as the authors of this work ha
with the Copyright, Designs and Patents Act

All rights reserved. No part of this publication may be reproduced, stored in or introduced into a retrieval system, or transmitted, in any form, or by any means (electronic, mechanical, photocopying, recording or otherwise) without the prior written permission of the publisher. Any person who does any unauthorized act

 relation to this publication may be liable for criminal prosecution and civil claims for damages.

Artwork by Jason Smith - www.macaruba.com

Copyright © 2020 Nigel L. Job and Lorna H. Rutter

All rights reserved.

ISBN 9798651139859

Table of Contents

Introduction 7
   Case Studies 15
   Example 1: Muldowney Legal 15
   Example 2: SubGaia Technology Ltd................................. 16
   Example 3: Acme Medical Inc. 18
Chapter 1 The Economics of Getting it Right or Wrong 20
   Assessment one: The economic impact of short-term unsuccessful hiring... 21
   Exercise one: Short term tenure impact on your business . 26
   Assessment two: The economic effect of incumbent underperforming employees 30
   Exercise two: Actual Performance V Performance Expectation 32
Chapter 2 A structured recruiting timetable for success 39
   A successful recruitment process...................................... 43
Chapter 3 High Performance Talent Focus: What Does 'Great' Look Like? 45
   What is diversity and why is it important? 48
   Exercise Three : Diversity and Inclusion 50
   Assessment 3 – What attracted your top performers? 51
   The Seven Indicators of High Performance Talent 53

Exercise Four: HPT Indicators Criteria Matrix 59

Assessment 4 - HPT Characteristics assessment chart 60

Chapter 4 The Importance of Employer Branding to attract High Performance Talent 65

Employee Value Proposition 68

How your employer brand can attract HPTs..................... 70

Measuring the effectiveness of Employer Branding 74

Exercise Five: What makes you a stand out employer? 79

Assessment 5 -Why would someone want to work for you & your company?... 80

Chapter 5 Business Needs Analysis 83

Understanding the key elements for a role 84

Learning from previous successes and mistakes................ 87

Summarizing the skills you need 89

Assessment six: Essential Skills.. 92

Exercise Six - Essential and desirable skills need analysis... 93

Writing an effective job description 95

Exercise Seven – Create a Job Description and Person Specification.. 101

Chapter 6 Candidate generation methods 103

Personal recommendation of hiring manager 106

Advertising 107

Social media 111

Hashtags 115

3

Company referral schemes 115
Internal Talent Acquisition (TA) team 116
Contingency recruitment companies 117
A retained search-consultancy partner 123
Temporary or contract/interim recruitment 126

Chapter 7 Short Listing, Interview and Assessment 129
Getting your management team(s) fit for purpose 129
CV reading and interpretation 133
Interviewing: preparation and interview skills 137
Function based questions 140
Performance based questions 141
HPT behavior differentiator questions 142
Exercise Eight – Role specific Interview questions 145
General interview skills: the 'first' interview 146
How to structure the interview 148
Second or subsequent Interviews 152
Additional methods of assessment 152
Reference Checking 157

Chapter 8 Hiring Success and Beyond 161
The offer 163
Post-hire quality process 166

Chapter 9 Staff Retention 170
Employee turnover 171
What is the tenure of staff who are leaving? 173

- Benefits of an exit interview 174
- Overall business performance 174
- Distribution of workload and productivity 175
- Employer brand and company image 176
- Team development... 177
- Is there ever a good time to have staff turnover? 177
- Staff turnover is low but it's the high performers who are leaving 179
- How to work with staff turnover to develop a high performance workforce 179
- Staff Retention Strategies 182

Epilogue.. 187

Summary 189

- ABOUT THE AUTHORS.. 191

ACKNOWLEDGMENTS

Our sincere thanks to all of the many people who have contributed to this book through their direct advice when we were researching. Also to all of our colleagues and clients and interviewees, past and present, who are the backbone of the inspiration for it.

Introduction

Recruitment and retention is key to your business growth. Whether we are in boom times or recession there is always a shortage of highly talented people at all levels. It is therefore an area of competition that your company should master in order to compete. And yet, "recruitment is broken", or so say many on the subject. What do they mean?

What they seem to mean is that the recruitment systems that companies use no longer work well; that candidates are treated poorly thereby damaging company employer brand; recruitment companies offer a poor and expensive service, and the results that employers get are inconsistent at best.

Is this a new phenomenon or has it always been thus?

The truth is that it probably always has been an area of human resource management that is in urgent need of a rethink. Most employers have not yet woken up to how bad their recruiting systems are, and how easily they can be improved. We use the word "systems" advisedly, because the real truth is most companies' approach to recruitment, selection and retention has anything but a systematic approach. What definitely *is* new is the plethora of approaches that companies can use to compete in this essential aspect of business growth. Genuine professional talent management is still in its embryonic stages in almost all companies. Recruitment is part of this, and of course one of the reasons why many consider recruitment to be "broken" is because there is little connection to retention, but more broadly a disconnect to other strategic areas of business.

Essentially, most recruiting and retention strategies used by companies are not in the least strategic.

They are fundamentally basic, badly integrated, and completely inadequate for the times that we live in. One of the fundamental reasons many companies' recruitment processes are not competing is because they are still employing and displaying attitudes that in reality were poor quality in the past, and completely inappropriate for the future, and their attempts to use modern technologies and methods are inept and amateurish, with a focus on completely the wrong metrics.

The current recruitment market is massively different from what it once was. This offers both opportunities and threats.

However, whether we look at the most modern methods of recruitment, or the more traditional, the root cause of the "broken recruitment" problem is a lack of focus on how to achieve a system of excellence that outperforms your competitors. Sadly, most employers do not know what good looks like, let alone "excellent" when it comes to hiring systems and processes, and the recruitment industry that ostensibly supports this effort does not, for the large part, have the guts to tell their clients what really needs to be done! There appears to be a non-symbiotic relationship between employers and the recruitment industry. In many, if not most cases, it is a relationship of supplier and purchaser rather than partner/advisor. If you are not receiving the recruitment service from either your internal or external partners that you think you deserve, it is not necessarily the case that recruitment is broken per se, but it is probably the case that YOUR recruitment systems are almost certainly sub-optimal.

One area that we will focus on heavily through this book is a clear philosophy to drive growth through your organization; make it your top strategic objective to *hire* and then *retain* **high performers**. A complaint from many hiring managers and HR professionals is that the quality of people they see is not meeting their expectations. Paradoxically, we will be encouraging you to be even more demanding in what you require. This might suggest you will make your task even harder, but this will not be the case if you follow the principles we outline in the following pages.

The market for high performers in all sectors is what recruiters refer to as "candidate led". This means that it is a "sellers-market" for their services, and, as already mentioned, it is really immaterial whether we are in a boom time or a recession. The reason for this is that in recession people are more cautious and less likely to move, so while there may be a larger number of people "between jobs", there will still be a very limited availability of high performers. If you are an employer that wants such high performing growth supercharging people, you are going to have to work hard to attract them, and if you do not, your competitors will take them instead!

The internet and social media platforms that are now part of our everyday lives mean that the way potential applicants interact with possible employers/recruiters and vice versa is completely different to what it was ten years ago. If you *are* still using the methods you used ten years ago, then as suggested a few paragraphs ago you are at a disadvantage. If you are adapting to the new environment, you need to understand how to do this optimally.

You will also be wise to understand the pressures that the new recruitment environment places on your existing staff. As it becomes easier for your best staff to be found by other employers, how do you ensure they are not tempted away? Afterall, you will not grow your business if having hired the right people you lose them in short order! It is certainly a broken system that hires great people and then lets them drift off before giving a clear return on investment.

One of the major obstacles to success is not only that many companies' line managers are unaware of the current dynamic in the recruitment market, but also that they have had minimal training or experience in how to interview and select. How broken is that? It is quite extraordinary that such a mission critical skillset for any manager or leader is left so much to chance. How many other management functions are carried out by individuals that have little training or instruction in that function? Not many perhaps.

If you are in charge of P&L for your business unit or company, and you are not a trained accountant, the likelihood is that you will have had at least received a training course in "finance for non-financial managers", or something of that type. If you need to do presentations to internal or external customers you will have been on presentation skills courses. And as for general leadership and management, it could be argued that you should be continually learning and developing yourself in this area if you have line management responsibility for others.

This book will help to address this gap, demonstrating best practice and most up to date principles for recruiting with a focus on accessing high performers and how to engage with them.

Interview and selection process improvement, when combined with a strong retention strategy is one of the most significant but straightforward management improvement processes that you can implement.

Whatever type of people you hire, whether they are people with a commercial target, such as lawyers, accountants or salespeople; or perhaps they are bench scientists working on a time critical project, the difference between poor performers and overperformers may well be the difference between overall success or failure of your business or organization.

The baseline quality of your team, and therefore much of its performance, is dependent on two straightforward factors: *how they are selected and how they are led*.

Leadership has had much written on it, and we will not be covering that here. However, how can you have a decent team to lead, if you haven't selected them well in the first instance? This book will take you on a journey that will demonstrate the value of a modern, outward looking and proactive selection process that will result in you hiring much higher-quality, higher-performing people and, subsequently, greater success for your organization. Those higher quality people we will refer to as High Performance Talent or HPT. This does not mean that we are only referring to geniuses, or super people. We are simply referring to those that are consistently at the top end of their professional capability when compared to their peer group.

Can all organizations aim at such groups?

Yes, definitely!

If you want to see increased productivity through improved talent there are a number of key elements that need to be grasped:

- Accessing High Performance Talent needs to be a key strategic objective of the organization that is prioritized to the very top of the leadership team, and "buy-in" achieved right through the organizational structure.

- People are not commodities, the highest quality people need to be competed for. The best candidates have the pick of employers, not the out of date attitude that believes it is the other way around.

- A robust process must be put in place to ensure that consistency is applied throughout the recruitment program, across the organization and outcomes are measured.

If the principles given here are followed, you will save many hours of lost time and lost productivity in the future, that would have been caused through taking the wrong approach, interviewing the wrong people and worse still, hiring the wrong people.

When these principles are applied, your recruitment processes will be far from broken or out of date, they will be high performance. High Performance Hiring processes will lead to High Performance Talent being attracted to your organization and supercharging its future growth.

Case Studies

To demonstrate how we can apply the processes to all types of hiring we are using a few fictional illustrative and disparate examples* that we will follow through the course of this book:

Example 1: Muldowney Legal

Muldowney Legal, (result of a recent Merger between Knight Murphy Kett LLP and Muldowney Knight LLP) is a fast growing Dublin based law firm with 82 partners, and over 600 employees, of which 345 are "fee earning" lawyers. They have subsidiary offices in London, Belfast and New York.

Their HR Director, Megan Doyle, has four big problems.

1. The firm has grown significantly in recent years and it has struggled to hire the fee earning lawyers to meet the needs of their ever growing client base.

2. Additionally, they now have an attrition rate for losing staff of all types that is double the average for other law firms in Dublin. They have gained an unfortunate reputation as a result.

3. Recent hires are underperforming targets in both total revenue per quarter and average hourly fee rate.

4. Their recruitment budget has been overspent by between 150 and 220% for the last three years.

The overall challenge is that the firm appears to be a victim of its own success, and the four problems are now hindering the company's profitability and growth plans. A change in HR strategy is clearly needed.

Example 2: SubGaia Technology Ltd

SubGaia Technology Ltd. (SGT) is an Adelaide, Australia based high growth software company that uses a technology similar to types of 3-D gaming for applications used in geological exploration of the deep sea-bed. It currently has eleven staff including the three founders; Kris Marne, John Kellogg and Trisha Brown. They are venture capital funded and in the last 18 months received a new round of funding that was over-subscribed and will enable the next phase of their product development and market release of their first product in the next five years.

In order to meet its growth plans and milestones promised to investors, SGT will need to employ a further thirty people. This will include, software developers, project managers and a marketing and business development department that is projected to require a minimum of five hires. They originally decided to take a "collegiate" approach to their hiring on the basis that they believe their "laid back" culture should not be adversely changed by new hires.

Immediately after receiving their funding they started their hiring process and originally decided that all new hires will need to be interviewed by all three Founders and four of the longest serving employees.

SGT has the following principle challenges with this growth plan:

- Whilst initially successful in the first few months, the first full 12 months of their recruitment program has not been as successful as they had hoped and they currently are significantly behind in hiring the number of people that they should have done by now.

- While SGT has a number of experienced non-executive directors, its three founders are PhD graduates with no previous industry experience prior to setting up SGT 5 years ago. Two of them are geophysicists and one a software engineer. None of them has had any hiring experience prior to two years ago.

- They did not originally have a HR Director as they felt they "know a good engineer when they see one", and general HR could be looked after by their office manager who is the partner to one of the founders. It was over a year after their funding round that they discovered this was not sustainable.

- They have looked to hire as many software engineers and the marketing people "through their network" where possible as they want to avoid "costly recruitment fees" and focus their cash on project milestones. This has proved effective in parts but it has been ineffective in hiring the volume of people required at the speed needed for their growth plans.

Example 3: Acme Medical Inc.

Acme Medical Inc. is a listed US manufacturer of hospital beds and patient-handling equipment (hoists, etc.). It is a medium-sized business with stable low percentage growth.
It is not a market leader in revenue size, but considers itself to be a leader in terms of the quality of its products.

It has a diverse workforce and fosters a culture of high performance, which is reflected by its strong stock-market record. It has worked hard to acquire a good employer brand, and its rating on Glassdoor (the predominantly US-centric website that compares employers) is positive.

It looks after its people and has a highly respected image in its home US market. Its global distribution is mixed-channel, with some direct sales and some that come through distributors.

It has a direct operation in a number of the key markets in Europe, including Germany, France, Italy, Spain, The Netherlands and the UK. It has recently acquired a high tech patient handling system company and has decided to expand its European operation, in particular Germany, France and The Netherlands to properly exploit this. Competition for this market in Europe is considerably tougher than the US, due to their being both a German and French manufacturer of similar products. The hiring responsibility will be divided between the US based

VPHR, Tim Brooker and the newly appointed European General Manager, Lena Rollinger.

Challenges:

- The company has very little brand awareness in Europe, particularly Germany.

- They have limited experience of hiring in Europe. Their European HR Manager is highly functional and not strategic.

- Their small existing sales team in Europe is stable, but very orientated to "order taking" type selling for the existing products.

- The existing sales team is in the lower quartile for salaries based on a recent salary survey.

As we navigate through the chapters in this book we will refer to the differing challenges for these three companies, and how they can apply the recruitment processes and structures we recommend to achieve success.

*These companies the individuals and events described are illustrative and fictional. Any resemblance to real companies or persons living or dead is unintentional and purely coincidental.

Chapter 1
The Economics of Getting it Right or Wrong

Before putting together a hiring and retention plan, it is beneficial to understand the economic benefit that such planning will bring. It is, in a sense, a simple Return On Investment. When you map out your process you will realize that to do this properly it will require a time and effort investment. As you progress through these recommendations it will become more than apparent that the time invested will not only result in considerable time ultimately saved, but also massive potential cost savings and productivity revenue improvements.

There has not yet, to our knowledge, been a definitive economic study looking at comparing the real 'cost of hire'. It is a clear truth that most people would realize that a poor recruitment decision can be very costly. Many organizations are too accepting of their poor hiring record, and little is done to fix it. Often, the wrong metrics are looked at, such as how they can reduce recruitment costs (which, in turn, inevitably results in poorer processes).

Fact: The best way to reduce recruitment costs is to make better decisions, resulting in a lower recruiting frequency!

We are going to provide you with strategies, processes and ideas that can change the shape of your teams, shift the way you approach the hiring process and, ultimately, give you employees that will have a serious impact on you as a hiring manager and on the growth and success of your organization.

Our advice to you is to not skip the assessments but to read, digest, STOP – and then take action. Carry out the assessments on your current team members and review their productivity over the last five years. Armed with this baseline information, make your way through the rest of the book with this knowledge in mind. If you do this, the contents of the book will be more powerful and specific to your needs. Then, you can be planning and developing as you go.

Assessment one: The economic impact of short-term unsuccessful hiring

The economic impact of unsuccessful hires that last less than 12 months can be assessed by looking at people who have short tenures after being hired by your organization over the last five years. It is a reasonable assumption that, in most organizations, a person that lasts less than 12 months is an uneconomic hire. In most cases this will lead to an underperformance for that job function and its related objectives for a considerable period, either through the incompetence of the bad hire, or through significant periods when the post is vacant.

It is important to look at the impact of hiring decisions on each uneconomic hire in terms of the performance of that role versus normal expectations. Different roles are easier to measure in terms of the economic impact of short term hires or underperformance than others. Positions that have revenue targets such as fee earning professionals such as lawyers, accountants, recruitment consultants or salespeople etc. are relatively easy to measure. It is a simple measure of the difference between target and actual revenue less the person's costs. With other roles it may be more complex. None-the-less you probably have a good understanding of some sort of productivity index for the staff that report to you. If you do not, this may be a good time to find out from your HR department whether they have such measures, and if not why not?!

If you have baseline metrics to work from you can identify expected work outputs. This should be relatively straightforward for roles that have specific quantifiable outputs in terms of projects.

In our example tech company, SGT, their project managers and engineers should have clear milestones to deliver. The tasks will be measurable and aligned to the company or organizational objectives with qualitative measurement also included.

Once you understand what the productivity expectation is, one can then understand what the value of standard performance is for that role, and what the contribution of that role should be over a time period of say, a year. It is worth noting that the effect of poor hiring decisions can be cumulative, as any new person is faced with the challenge of turning round the previous lack of activity in the affected post. If a post has had more than one unsuccessful hire in succession, it will take good management and a very talented and resourceful employee to get things back on track!

Example:

Let us therefore consider Muldowney Legal's attempt at the beginning of last year to hire a Commercial Property lawyer. This was a replacement for someone that had left to go to a competitor. It was considered to be highly urgent to find a replacement, but little was done until the individual actually left. She had been a well-regarded successful lawyer consistently billing €400k a year in fees, against a target of around €375k.

One of the partners knew someone who appeared to have the right skills from a previous firm that he had worked at. The individual was interviewed, and while he appeared highly technically able there were concerns about cultural fit and attitudes. These concerns were overridden by the head of department, Pat Halliday, who felt he wanted someone quickly and was also pleased to avoid a recruitment fee, and the appointment was made, all within the space of 6 weeks.

It was all considered a great success until about 4 weeks in when it was observed that the individual had major interpersonal challenges, which resulted in consultations with the new hire which were interspersed with a number of periods off sick. He was ultimately dismissed after 10 weeks having recorded only 15 billable hours work.

A further month of hiring inactivity took place due to high work load of Pat Halliday (who was picking up some of the departed person's workload) and holidays. Megan Doyle, the HR Director, was also overworked having been focused on the implementation of an integration project following the company merger.

Two existing clients of the firm, who had been looked after by the previous incumbent announced they were changing lawyers.

Pat Halliday then sent the job description to five Dublin based contingency recruitment firms. They requested time to speak with him, but he protested he was too busy and instructed them to work from the old job description. Very few candidates were forthcoming and Pat told Megan that the recruiters on the Preferred Supplier List were useless and they had now lost another 6 weeks.

Megan recommended that their normally most successful recruiter, Dublin Legal Recruitment Ltd., was invited into the office and was able to be fully briefed by her and Pat. The recruiter was then given three weeks exclusivity and presented two very strong candidates. The post was filled after a five stage interview process over a period of 5 weeks, and the candidate was on a 3 month notice period from their existing employer.

The total time from the departure of the previous incumbent was almost 50 weeks before the new person started. Only approximately 20% of the original existing business had been picked up by the other lawyers in the team, the rest lost.

Irrespective of billing loss in the early days of the newest hire, it is clear to see a substantial loss in revenue due to a failure of Muldowney Law's recruitment process that initially led to a bad short term hire. This was then compounded by poor response to that situation that was ultimately corrected many weeks later than necessary.

Loss of revenue against company target due to this uneconomic hire was approximately €300k. This example was only one of several failed hires that the firm has had in the last 2 years. The revenue lost runs into millions of euros.

Exercise one: Short term tenure impact on your business

1.   Work out the number of hires in the last five years that have lasted less than 12 months. (If you have a moderate or large workforce and you have had no hiring disasters, give yourself and your HR team a pat on the back!)

2.   Discover whether there are any reliable datasets or indicators showing average tenure in your industry to see if you are above average or below average for these types of short-tenured hires. (If this number of short-tenure hires is well below the industry average, you might be less concerned. However, if it is well in excess of the average, it is clear that you are losing a lot of productivity unnecessarily due to poor recruiting processes).

3.   Investigate or estimate the productivity value difference between expected productivity and actual performance for each team member. Assuming that expected productivity would have been achieved by a core performing team member, you now have a reasonable estimate as to how much suboptimal hiring decisions are costing you per year.

It is relatively straightforward to calculate the cost of short tenures for commercial people such as sales or professional fee-earning staff such as lawyers. It becomes slightly more complex for non-commercial staff, where it is more challenging to place a monetary value on their contribution as they may not have a direct impact on revenue generation. However their overall impact on company productivity through efficiencies/inefficiencies may be significant.

If the objective of a particular role is to enable others to more efficiently focus on their own roles then the resultant effect can be in someone completing a project late or perhaps generating less revenue. It is therefore sensible to consider the Return On Investment (ROI) for any role hired, of any seniority, and their Productivity Contribution to the company's growth and success.

Example:
SGT seek to employ an Administrator to support the general business administration. Unfortunately as there was little structure in place, and the person hired believed that promises that were made at interview were not fulfilled, they left after only 3 months of employment. In order to work out the financial impact of this short tenure we need to look at two areas; the gains from the investment and the cost of the investment.

This would be calculated by:

Gains from the investment (GI) - Cost of the investment (CI)

= ROI of the Employee

For each employee you firstly need to assign a monetary value in relation to their expected output. With every hire that you take on there will have been a reason for doing so. The founders estimated that they were each using up a total of approximately 50 days a year for general administration. They also anticipated that this administrative workload was likely to increase exponentially.

They have calculated that their own value to the business on average is A$1250 per day each.

SGT hired an administrator and had calculated that delegating the day to day administrations, diary management, logistics, sifting through recruitment applications and managing procurement meant that the founders could recoup their time to reinvest in other areas of the business which was going to have significant impact on the growth of the business.

Annual gains from this hire:

GI= A$1250 x 150 (working days) = A$187 500

Now let's look at the cost of the investment:

Hiring costs (hired through a local agency)	A$8000
Salary & benefits	A$55,000
Training and onboarding costs	A$5000

Total annual investment cost = A$68000

Therefore the Return On Investment is:

ROI= (GI) A$187500 − (CI) A$68000 = A$119500

The Administrator in this scenario makes a Productivity Contribution of approximately A$10 000 per month. As with all roles it will take a certain amount of time before the new hire acquires company specific knowledge to reach an optimum level. With this type of role it might be assumed that the person will reach this level on about month 3.

Having someone in post means their productivity contribution is A$10,000 per month, or the opposite if you don't have them. You would be losing that productivity contribution by not having someone in post as the founders will continue to pick up this function which means they cannot put their skill set into 'other' areas where they themselves will be more productive. You then need to consider the costs to re-hire and find yourself with double the recruitment costs, onboarding and training costs, plus the losses associated with the post being vacant longer than required. Conversely a good hire will reach their optimum Productivity Contribution more quickly and overachieve against this measure.

This type of calculation gives us a greater understanding of having such a post vacant for any extended period of time, and the disruption that can be caused when a person leaves after such a short amount of time, as shown in this example.

Assessment two: The economic effect of incumbent underperforming employees

We were recently speaking with a CEO of a mid-sized company with a sales force of around 120 people and asked what the difference in sales performance was between their top performing salespeople (their HPT) and their poorest. The results were not really surprising. Essentially, it was that low performers were hitting around 60% of their targets. The top 10% were hitting 150%.

Assume, then, that at Acme Medical their salespeople take an average of 12 months to really get up to speed after they have been hired, and that they have a target in their second year of $1M per annum.

Their bottom 10% are hitting only 60% of target, or $600,000

Their top 10% are hitting 150% of target, or $1,500,000

This kind of difference is not uncommon.

Therefore, in this example, the difference between a really good hire and a really bad one at Acme Medical is a massive $900k in lost revenue in year two (per territory) alone! Even when comparing core performers who hit their target and a high performer, we are looking at a difference of $500k.

A bad hiring decision instead of a good one will cost Acme Medical between $400k and $900k per territory, per year!

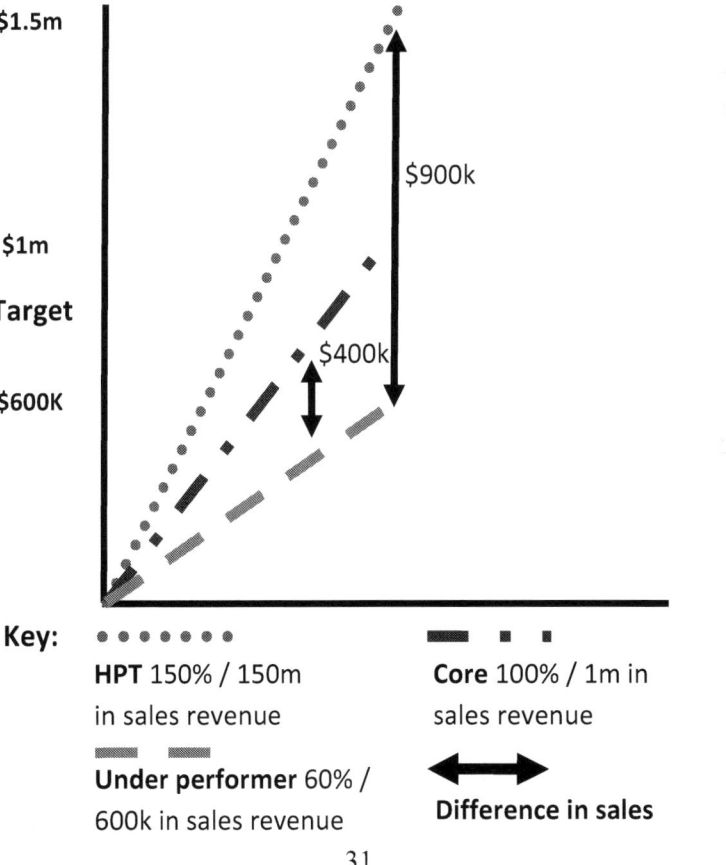

Exercise two: Actual Performance V Performance Expectation

This exercise will require you giving a monetary value to your individual team members performance as described on pages 22 and 23. This does not need to be precise because the exercise is largely indicative.

Look at the last two years' performance versus your team's performance objectives.

Exercise 2: Part 1. - Calculate and analyze the performance figures for your top 10% of performers who have been with the company for a minimum period of two years. Do the same for your bottom 10% of performers.

Exercise 2: Part 2. - Assess any factors that may exaggerate these differences that are beyond the control of the individual. You may wish to make allowances for any differentials caused by unusual conditions or different levels of training or relative tenure that may have exaggerated their performance either negatively or positively.

Clearly it would not be reasonable, all things being equal, to expect an individual who has been in post for only 24 months to be achieving similar levels of productivity to someone that has been with you for 10 years.

Hopefully, however, the productivity expectations that you have set your people already reflect this. If they do not, you may want to review why not and to ask whether this may be a contributory factor to their underperformance.

Equally, if you believe a strong performance may be the result of activities or events that have not entirely resulted due to the person's own initiatives, you may need to apply a negative adjustment to the results. Applying a negative adjustment is not an exact science, but it will give you an overall picture of where you should be taking action.

Exercise 2: Part 3. - Take the expected performance figures and adjust to reflect variations, then look at the combined above-performance figures achieved by your top 10% .

NB: This is not an exercise for the identification of poor performers and we are not advocating that such individuals should necessarily be disciplined or dismissed. A far more in-depth assessment of the reasons for underperformance would be needed for this purpose.

This exercise is fundamentally about understanding the economic differences between overperformance and underperformance, and the desirability of orientating one's business in a way that facilitates the pursuit of high performers.

Example

Let us return to Dublin to the apparently luckless Megan Doyle. She feels quite stressed. She is actually an exceptional HR leader. She has a background in HR from one of the world's leading accountancy and management consulting firms that was many times the size of Muldowney Law. She was brought into the firm three years ago based on many promises that have turned out to be, well, somewhat exaggerated! However, she is not a quitter and is determined to sort out the significant HR challenges that the firm is facing.

Her recent figures that she has uncovered with considerable difficulty from the heads of department demonstrate that of the 300 or so lawyers that she has gathered data on who have been in the company 2 years or longer, 30% are significantly underperforming against their quarterly targets, 30 % are regularly below, and 30% meeting them. 10% are consistently above target.

She considers the targets against data she has, comparing them to targets for specialisms within other leading law firms in Dublin. She also looks at the distribution of performance to target against tenure that shows little or no correlation, thereby demonstrating the targets are fair.

Her findings are as follows:

The Top 10% of performers: average annual differential between performance and expected performance (target):

PLUS €60k

The bottom 10% of performers: average annual differential between performance and expected performance (target):

MINUS €90k

She is therefore able to demonstrate that the difference between a high performer and a low performer is a massive €150k revenue!

In Megan's case it is recommended that she carry our further analysis on this information and work out:

1. What can we learn from the high performers?

2. Who needs to be upskilled?

3. Who is not being properly managed?

4. Challenging though the question may be; who perhaps should have never been hired in the first place?

Exercise 2: Part 4. - Apply the question as shown in our example above to the findings from your own company and team analysis. What is this telling you?

It is entirely possible that you may do the exercises and discover that your losses due to short-tenure hires and underperformers are either minimal or acceptable to you, particularly if you feel that this figure compares well to the industry average. However, we rarely come across companies that would not do well to radically improve their hiring processes, particularly where a drive towards hiring high potentials and high performers is the objective.

Other factors to consider when reviewing the impact of short term tenure and underperformance is the costs to hire someone new, these are likely to include:

- Recruitment fee.

- Administration time to write job description, person specification, job advert.

- Advertising costs.

- Administration time to review all the applications and shortlist.

- Interview time and any interview costs (eg. Travel, room hire, assessment center).

- Putting the new hire through an induction program.

- Training costs.

- Management time to onboard the new starter.

- Additional support over the first 6-8 weeks of joining the company.

All of these factors can be assigned a monetary value which will allow you to work out how much has been invested in hiring the person in addition to their salary and benefits.

The fundamental purpose of the exercises in this chapter are to demonstrate the potential cost of not observing best practice when recruiting people. Therefore, the relatively small amount of time spent ensuring that best practice is followed will have a massive impact, producing a return on investment that will, as we said previously, greatly exceed many other business-process improvements upon which you could embark.

At the end of this chapter you should now have an understanding of:

- The economic impact of poor hiring decisions.

- How to calculate the financial impact a short tenure can have on your team and organizational targets.

- How to calculate an indicative ROI of an employee and the productivity contribution an employee can have on an organization.

- The difference between an underperforming employee and HPT and therefore why it is desirable to change your hiring strategy to attract high performing individuals.

- What costs need to be considered when hiring and onboarding.

- The best way to reduce recruitment costs is to make better hiring decisions resulting in lower recruiting frequency.

Chapter 2
A structured recruiting timetable for success

In The 7 Habits of Highly Effective People, Stephen Covey says 'start with the end in mind'. To prepare a timetable for success it is best to start with the time by which it seems reasonable to get the person on board and then work backwards from there. If you are in a geographical area where it is common for people to have three months' notice, you will need to factor that in. You will need to decide when you are doing second interviews, first interviews and initial shortlist discussions, as well as estimating a realistic period of candidate generation.

If a project manager can be assigned to the project, then they can make sure that any participants in the process give their availability. If you are using a good recruiter they can help you plan this timetable. Good planning will not only help the process from an internal perspective, it also looks much more professional to the candidates. The best candidates are impressed by organizations that are professional and organized. Such people are also often time-poor. If you are able to tell them at the start of the process what they can expect, this will present the right image as well as make the process run to time.

Multiple hires can require quite complex project management skills. If there are a range of different roles, it is first worth considering which roles you need to hire first. If you are hiring a whole team, such as at SGT in our example, you will need to perhaps consider focusing on the most mission critical first, but simultaneously considering the average "time-to-hire" for each role. A more senior role may take considerably longer to resource, and then may have a longer process "runway" (more interviews) and a longer notice period to wait out.

Also bear in mind the availability of your interviewing team. This is often one of the greatest constraining factors on time-to-hire. It is best if each interviewer schedules time for interviewing with flexibility to be available when the candidates are available. This is explored further in chapter 7.

Things to consider when planning you timetable:
- When do you want them to start and work backwards
- Notice period
- Interviewer availability
- Any holidays scheduled
- Can they start even if the reference isn't back?
- What information needs to be available to candidates and interviewers

There is really no magic bullet for hiring HPTs; there can be no perfect system that will guarantee we will always pick winners. What we can do is radically increase our chances of acquiring such people and reduce or possibly eradicate our chances of hiring general low-performing charlatans and the indolent.

As with so many things in life, if you want to produce consistent and reliable results you need to put together a process that is similarly consistent; one that is robust and resistant to irrational leaps of faith and gut instinct–driven hiring decisions.

We are not suggesting that gut instinct should be ignored. A human resources contact once told us that in her opinion, gut instinct was a useful natural mechanism that uses many small signals that you have learned over a lifetime to alert you to issues. This makes a lot of sense.

Therefore, while hiring decisions largely based on instinct should be avoided, concerns should not. If you feel concerned, further investigation may be warranted.

A good process that will find, attract, and retain the very best applicants will involve the following:

- A structured timetable for success, with a project manager assigned to 'own' the process.

- An outstandingly effective candidate-generation model.

- An assessment system for CVs/resumes.

- Fully prepared and skilled interviewers and assessors for all stages (particularly for the early 'recruiter' stage).

- Additional assessment tools orientated to HPT identification.

- A well-informed and highly skilled negotiator to support the offer.

- An outstanding and inviting onboarding process.

- Post-hire monitoring, coaching and mentoring that is orientated toward HPTs. These may well continue for a long time into the person's employment, if not indefinitely.

A successful recruitment process

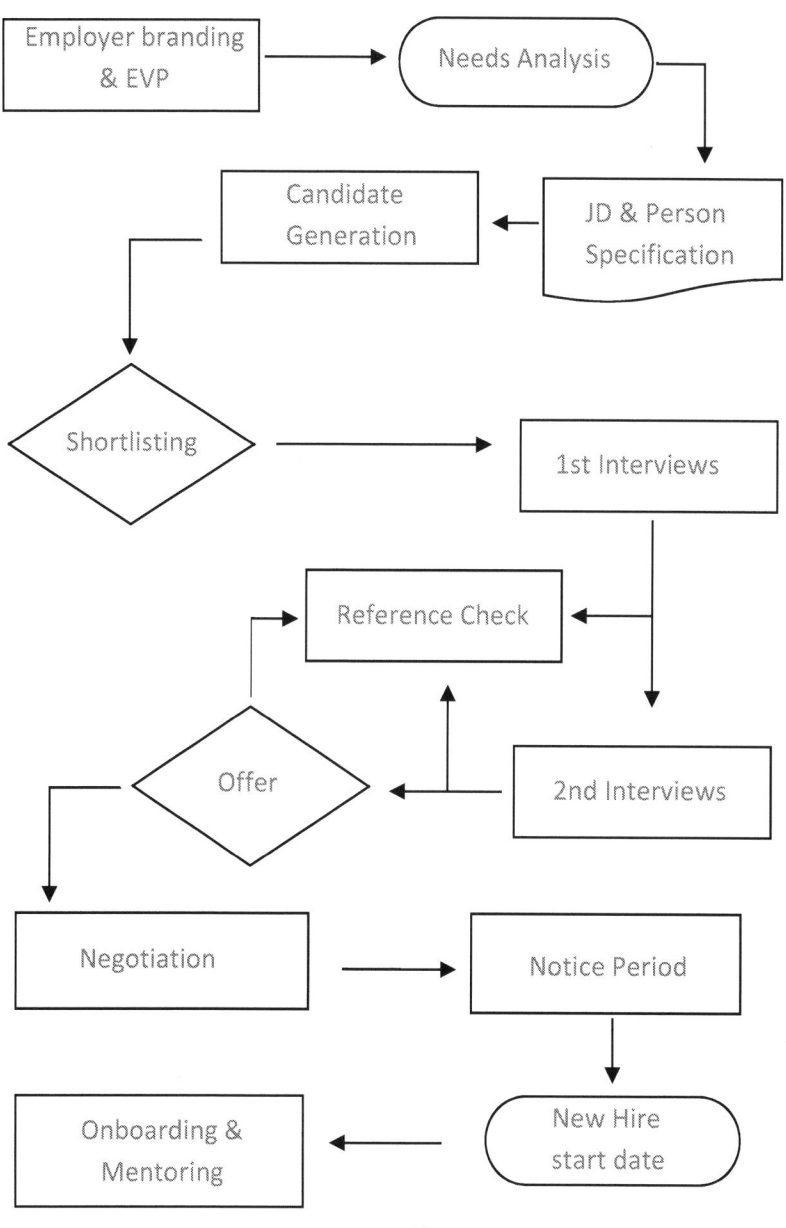

```
Employer branding & EVP → Needs Analysis
                            ↓
Candidate Generation ← JD & Person Specification
    ↓
Shortlisting → 1st Interviews
                    ↓
         Reference Check
         ↑           ↑
       Offer ← 2nd Interviews
         ↓
Negotiation → Notice Period
                    ↓
Onboarding & Mentoring ← New Hire start date
```

43

As we move through the remaining chapters of the book we will explore each of the different elements of the recruitment process and discuss how we can ensure best practice with a HPT focus can be accomplished to achieve your hiring and ultimately your business objectives.

In chapter 2 we have discovered:

- The recruitment process flow in any organization is relatively the same, the differences occur with the implementation, structure and approach to that process.

- Why you should always start with the end in mind. When do you want/need someone to start in the role and then what needs to happen and when to make this a reality.

- What areas need to be considered when planning your recruitment process/program to achieve your hiring goals.

Let's begin in Chapter 3 looking at High Performance Talent focus.

Chapter 3
High Performance Talent Focus: What Does 'Great' Look Like?

If our objective is to increase the productivity of the company and supercharge growth through hiring high performers, how are we going to get more such people into our organization?

If there is such a significant difference between high performers and low performers it makes considerable sense to attempt to attract those that demonstrate characteristics of high performance in terms of what that means for your company. This does not necessarily mean that all your hires will then fall into this category, but it does mean it will "raise the bar" resulting in higher expectations and an overall improvement in not only your recruiting process, but by extension your company performance and growth .

'Talent' is an overused word in the modern workplace. When one thinks of talent, one might think of Usain Bolt or Serena Williams, Kiri Te Kanawa or Led Zeppelin.

After all, a dictionary definition states that 'talent' means 'a special ability that allows someone to do something well', which seems pretty accurate. It certainly should not mean 'any candidate will do, so long as it doesn't cost us too much to find them', which is sadly too often what the word means in modern corporate recruitment. Therefore, because of the misuse of the word talent, we choose to refer to the people you want as High Performance Talent or HPT, as mentioned earlier. We need to select and identify HPTs for your team.

What is the difference between HPT selection and HPT identification?

HPT selection is the inclusion or exclusion of those with (or without) the current ability to be highly successful, as defined by your well-considered criteria (more on this later).

HPT identification is the prediction of future performance against those same criteria. People that meet this criterion are often described in many organizations as 'high potentials'.

Both of these factors, selection and identification, should be included if you intend to build a team of HPTs. You are looking for those that have the core capability now, and the potential to be there in the future.

What does a great person in your sector 'look' like? What could they look like?

This question may be risky! Sometimes, hiring managers' may be attracted to applicants that are likable, keen, or often are most like them. The first two factors may be preferable, even highly desirable in people who have customer interaction, but they are not necessarily essential in all roles. "Being most like them" is quite definitely undesirable. Tom Peters once said 'some companies hire people who look the same, sound the same, wear the same suit, went to the same college, did the same degree, and then wonder why they are not a hotbed of success and innovation!'

Returning to our example company SGT, you will recall that we referred to how they are very proud of what they see as their culture. A mistake often made in start-up companies is to confuse culture with uniformity, or conformity with the founder members. Conformity to a common set of values or sense of direction and purpose is good, but making your hiring decisions based on whether someone went to the same university or school or likes the same sports team or common interest is not. Inexperienced leaders often make the mistake of thinking that culture is exclusive rather than inclusive. One of the many errors that SGT made in the first year of their hiring campaign was to reject candidates that were a little challenging to their way of thinking. They excused the rejection of these candidates by suggesting they were "not a cultural fit". Many of them probably were a cultural fit, had the company at that time properly understood what the culture was. In reality they had never ascertained what their culture was. When their HR Director, Vince Price came on board he discovered all three founders had differing ideas as to what the culture was!

This was subsequently corrected and a "values statement" was crafted to guide their understanding of what their culture is. It enabled them to better hire for talent and led to much greater diversity and creativity in their teams.

What is diversity and why is it important?

Diversity in the workplace context refers to the way that people from different backgrounds and perspectives are able to participate together to achieve common goals.

By creating and offering an attractive workplace that is diverse forms creative and vibrant cultures. It provides management and peer groups with a greater understanding of the needs of employees, each other and customers. Bringing together the minds of a diverse group of people develops innovation and encourages creativity at a different level. It is fair to say that a team from a diverse background is going to have a broader range of experiences to draw from and therefore seeking methods and ways to attract this talent will without a doubt enhance your business and position you as a company to work for, work with, and buy from. According to research by The Work Foundation good diversity policies result in:

- improved performance
- improved employer image
- improved brand awareness
- improved ability to respond and change through creativity and innovation
- innovative approaches to products
- a reflective diversity that makes customers feel at home.

For an HPT, this type of organization that encourages and values a diverse and inclusive culture is going to be very attractive to them. It is therefore important as part of your employer branding that this is shared in order to attract high performers to your organization. (See chapter 4, Employer Branding.)

Exercise Three : Diversity and Inclusion

Answer these questions about your organization's diversity and inclusion strategy and think about how this can be used to attract high performing talent.

- What is your organizations D&I strategy?

- How does D&I contribute to delivery of business performance goals?

- How are D&I considerations incorporated into strategic decision making to achieve company goals?

- How are leaders held accountable for D&I results?

- What mechanisms are in place to monitor and then respond to what is working – and what is not?

- How effectively do D&I programs create a more inclusive environment?

- What methods of D&I are or could be used to attract high performing talent?

Assessment 3 – What attracted your top performers?

Explore what it was about your company's D&I strategy that attracted your top performers to work for your organization in the first place, and what can you learn from this to attract more?

If you are unclear on how to answer any of these questions or can only give vague answers then work here needs to be done.

- What have you learnt?
- What action should you take with this information?
- How can this information be used to attract top talent
- Is anything missing or areas of improvement?
- Who do you need to involve to develop this further?

We have discussed the reasons why D&I is important and the benefits to both employers and employees alike. There are some simple steps as part of your talent attraction methods that can be taken to appeal to a wider talent pool of candidates whilst at the same time removing the chances of unconscious biases during the hiring process.

These include:

- Highlight on your website the inclusion policy, and highlight this in any job adverts.

- Check your advert, job description and person specification uses inclusive language.

- When applicants come for interviews make sure D&I forms part of the interview and they are made aware of how this is an important aspect of working for your company.

- Use a number of people to carry out the interviews at the different stages of the process.

- Use the company values at all stages of the hiring process. Value-based hiring means you are identifying and bringing people on board who share those values and feel more on board and committed to the organization.

Diversity is not a politically correct agenda inspired by faceless bureaucrats in government offices; it is a driving mechanism for high performance. Not only does it help deliver performance, it also attracts and retains high performers. It is perhaps common sense to say that top performers who are in minority groups will likely be repelled by a lack of diversity.

When we look for the answer to the question raised at the start of this chapter raises, 'What does/could a great person in your sector look like?' it needs to have consideration for everything we have already discussed in this chapter so far but also be focused on the attributes that can be identified as leading to high performance. If you already have a team, it is worth looking at the traits of the top performers and those of the middling core and underachievers.

Over the next few pages we shall explore the seven indicators of High Performance Talent and why identifying these traits in anyone you are planning to hire will lead to significant performance improvement and supercharged growth.

The Seven Indicators of High Performance Talent

Competitiveness
HPTs compete with others and themselves, though not normally in a crass way. They see an objective and want to meet it or beat it. Rarely are they worried about being measured; in fact, they embrace such measurement. They are often not satisfied with their performance even if it is outstanding; they want to get even better as they have very high standards. They will know their most recent performance and will be able to clearly articulate their achievements at and outside work. They do not allow their competitiveness to make them arrogant. Their drive to be

better and their emotional intelligence keeps them grounded. Their lack of showy arrogance perhaps makes them more likely to be listened to by colleagues and customers and thereby will become a trusted advisor. This also normally makes them good team players, as they treat their colleagues with respect.

Intelligence
For most professional roles, high performing employees have a measure of intelligence that puts them in the upper quartile for their peers. This may be measured in IQ, emotional intelligence (EQ) and adaptability quotient (AQ). For some highly technical roles high IQ scores may be very important, and in others, particularly where a large amount of team interaction is required strong emotional intelligence will enable them to understand the problems of others often before that person knows that they have a problem. This type of intelligence is often demonstrated by the fact that they are highly articulate and persuasive, but they are even better at listening. They use these abilities to give colleagues and customers options that no-one else has thought of. They are able to demonstrate a continuously open mindset as opposed to a closed mindset and have the ability to adapt to and thrive in an environment of change. This is also characterized by a strong element of autodidacticism (an ability to teach themselves). They like to learn, often their own way, by reading articles, books, training and online learning. They are continuously looking for ways to challenge and improve themselves. They are

also normally comfortable with technology and are adept at using it to further enhance their performance.

Communication skill

High performers are almost always excellent communicators. The ability to communicate with internal and external stakeholders is a highly desirable quality in any team member. It is all very well being technically brilliant at something but if your ability to communicate your ideas is less than optimal, it makes your ability to be a high performer somewhat limited.

Much is spoken about personality profiles and in particular the introvert/extrovert spectrum, and its effect on communication style. Psychologists will tell us that while most of us have a preference for either extroversion or introversion, this is simply a preference; i.e. It does not entirely dictate how we must behave. Therefore, those that are able to adapt their style to the circumstance they find themselves in give themselves a performance advantage. These are individuals that are able to be somewhat extrovert when required, or more considered and introverted in different circumstances. This is particularly valuable when considering people with a commercial responsibility.

It was discovered by Adam Grant of The Wharton School that the 'ambivert' personality type (people with a mix of extroversion and introversion in their personality) correlate with the highest-performing salespeople. Contrary to accepted stereotypes, super-confident extrovert characteristics are therefore not a reliable predictor of high sales performance, any more than people who are excellent high performing software developers need necessarily be introverted . Whatever the individual's personality preferences, the ability to communicate with different people with differing personality types and differing motivations is a capability that leads to high performance.

Resilience
HPTs show remarkable resilience through their ability to bounce back from rejection and disappointment. Someone who is resilient has a level of sheer determination and could be described as a solution-finder; they will find another way round any road block to overcome a problem and will not let it hold them back. They understand that the problem is not going to fix itself and they have the ability to recover quickly from a tough or difficult situation. They do not dwell on something that is not going their way or going wrong. A higher level of resilience can be seen in people who recognize that they may need to call-in other resources and people in order to overcome a challenge.

Ethics
Top-performers are not as ruthless in their personal desire for success as many people may think. They are normally highly ethical and have a strong moral compass.
Such people have a strong desire to make a difference and truly believe that what they are contributing is going to

bring value to another person or maybe even society in general. They will not compromise on their values, and would rather resign their position than follow a path that would cause them to not be true to what they believe in.

Passion

HPTs love what they do and they often don't see work as 'work'; rather, they see at as part of who they are. Passion is not something that can be feigned, it is built from within. This is reflected in every process into which HPT enters into.

Drive

High performers are, probably above all things, highly driven individuals. In Jeff Haden's excellent "The Motivation Myth" he notes that high achievers generally set themselves a great goal and then set in place a great process to get there. They then put the end goal to the back of their mind and focus on that process. This is what drives their motivation and continues to feed their progress. Fundamentally, high achievers know what they want to get, but more importantly they figure out a way to get there. If someone says at interview "I want to be a millionaire", or "I want your job", ask them what their plan would be to acieve that.

One of the notable aspects of the seven indicators of HPT is that they are completely non-prejudicial on matters of diversity. Protected groups are not in any way at a disadvantage if you look for these traits across all candidates. You are equally likely to find all these attributes in suitable people irrespective of culture, ethnicity, orientation, disability, age, or gender.

In summary, an HPT could be described as; an intelligent, articulate person, who is highly competitive without being brash and arrogant, who has a passion for what they do, and has a focus on improving themselves and their results.

Exercise Four: HPT Indicators Criteria Matrix

Using the indicators criteria chart on the next page, identify HPT indicators within your own team.

1. Make a list of all the people in your team.

2. For indicative purposes, estimate how well you think they match the HPT criteria?

3. How well do the high scorers match actual performance?

   Please note, in order to undertake a genuinely objective analysis you will need to use properly formulated psychometric and aptitude tests. For the purpose of this exercise you will need to use a certain amount of objectivity because you are looking to gain an overall picture of your team rather than a detailed analysis of individuals.

Assessment 4 - HPT Characteristics assessment chart

Give each of your team members a score out of 10 (where 10 is the highest) according to how well you think they meet these measures (example score chart of next page).

Competitiveness:
Complete lack of competitive edge 1/10
Competes with themselves and others, high competitive 10/10

Intelligence: Estimate a score out of 10 for intelligence quotient (IQ), emotion quotient (EQ) and adaptability quotient (AQ). Combine the scores and take the average score.

Communication:
Lacks communication skills 1/10
Excellent communication and listening skills 10/10

Resilience: The ability bounce back and keep a positive frame of mind. Give a score out of 10.

Ethical: Highly Ethical and has a strong moral compass. Give a score out of 10.

Passionate: Demonstrates a natural 'love' for the work that they do. Give a score out of 10.

Drive: Has clearly defined goals and knows how they are going to achieve them. Give a score out of 10.

The seven indicators of High Performance Talent

Complete the below chart using the guidance notes to guide you with the scoring (1 being low and 10 being high).

Employee Name	Competitiveness Complete lack of competitive edge (1) / Highly competitive with themselves & others (10)	Intelligence Estimate a score for IQ, EQ & AQ. Combine & give score between (1-10)	Communication Lack of communication skill (1) / Excellent communication & listening skill (10)	Resilience Ability to bounce back & Keep positive (1-10)	Ethical Highly ethical & has strong moral compass (1-10)	Passionate Demonstrates a natural 'love' for the work that they do (1-10)	Drive Clearly defined goals & knows how they are going to achieve (1-10)
Name							
Name							
Name							
Name							

Having completed the assessment chart, answer the following questions:

How well do the individuals in your team match the above HPT indicators?

_____
_____
_____
_____
_____

If you have individuals in your team who clearly share these indicators, what are you going to do to keep them and make sure that they have the opportunity to shine and make the most of themselves?

_____
_____
_____
_____
_____

What can you learn from your HPT that you can use to train others?

_____
_____
_____
_____
_____

What other criteria do you think needs to be added to the list to reflect your top performers (if any)?

_____
_____
_____
_____
_____

What can you learn from your existing team that will allow you to identify what you want and don't want from your next hire?

_____
_____
_____
_____
_____

Through this chapter we have explored the following areas:

- Understanding your own company culture

- Why diversity in the workplace has a positive impact on the hiring and retention of HPT.

- The 7 key indicators to use when assessing if an application is HPT.

- How to use the assessment tool to review your current team against the HPT criteria.

- How to use your analysis of your team to retain HPT employees and identify traits in them that can be used in future hiring.

Chapter 4
The Importance of Employer Branding to attract High Performance Talent

Attention to your employer brand and the exercise on page 80 – What makes you a stand out employer? will give you a head start. High performers are, by their nature, more interested in company performance than their 'also-ran' colleagues are. They generally take pride in themselves and in their organizations and the people with whom they associate. If they get the impression that a company by whom they are being interviewed cares little for its reputation and lacks professionalism, they will not be interested. Conversely, they will be highly attracted to organizations that do care about their company reputation.

Additionally, they will be impressed by interviewers who know what they need for a role and who are able to demonstrate this through documentary evidence and process.

Throughout this chapter we will look at why employer branding is so important, how this can help to attract HPT to your organization and ultimately how you become an employer of choice.

At the very outset it essential that the company mission and values are clearly defined. You need to do more than just have them posted on the noticeboard by the watercooler or stuck on the intranet. It needs to be communicated and practiced at every opportunity. This includes talent acquisition, learning & development, external and internal negotiations, performance management and appraisals. Feedback needs to occur every day to create a culture with a common cause. Anyone that comes into contact with the organization should be able to get a true sense of what the organizational culture is like because the organization is run by their values.

When thinking about talent acquisition specifically then considering what your image in the employment market is, is absolutely essential.

What is your impression to external stakeholders? How do your competitors view you? Are you a market leader, or as a new disruptive entrant? The most expensive, mid-range or bargain-basement? Are you service-orientated or biased towards technological benefits? It is really important that you consider this honestly.

If your company has no significant brand presence (this might be the case for our start-up example SGT), is not renowned for high-quality services or products, or even, as is the case with our example Muldowney Law, a somewhat negative reputation as an employer, you need to think about how you are going to compensate for this when trying to attract the best people possible. A large part of the answer to this is to develop an effective "employer brand".

An employer brand makes a significant difference in all sectors and to all roles during the hiring process, and this is not something that is necessarily limited to the big corporates; small companies can develop excellent employer brands that make employees choose such companies over and above the larger more well-known employers.

Put simply, a well-developed employer brand can:

- Affect an applicant's decision to accept or reject a job offer.

- Mean that your company has less requirement to be in a damaging and costly salary "arms-race" with the competition as candidates and employees recognize that it isn't just money that counts.

- Assist with employee retention.

- Ensure people speak positively about your company, having a positive effect in all areas of your business.

Positive employer brand not only affects you and your employees, but also the development and growth of your business.

Many have developed employee branding statements which are displayed on their website, examples include:

Hubspot – "We're building a company people love. A company that will stand the test of time, so we invest in our people and optimize for your long term happiness"

Google – "Do cool things that matter"

L'Oreal – "Lead the future of beauty. When you love your work and the people you work with, amazing things can happen".

Employee Value Proposition

A fundamental element of any employer branding policy is the development of an employee value proposition (EVP). We strongly recommend that if your company does not have a company stated EVP you should at least develop one for your team. An EVP is the psychological agreement that describes what an employer expects from their employees and what an employee can expect in return. An EVP should answer one fundamental question for potential employees:

'Why should I work for this organization, and why should I stay?'

If an EVP is to be created in a formal way, clearly it also needs to be followed through. The five key elements that should be incorporated into your EVP are:

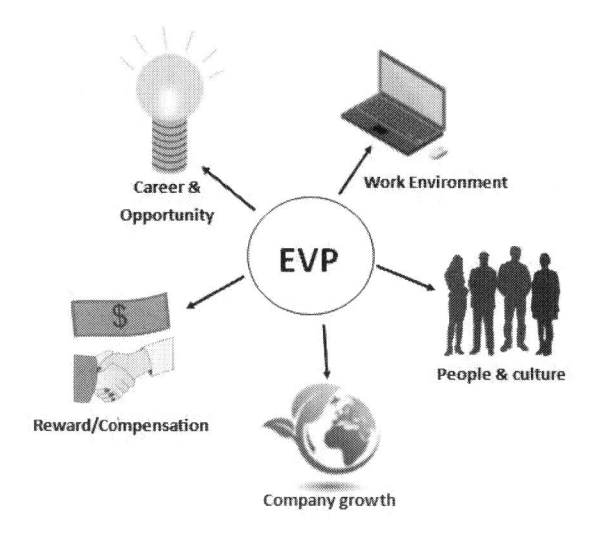

Career & Opportunity

Work Environment

EVP

Reward/Compensation

People & culture

Company growth

Some of the best and most successful companies will have this information displayed on their website and it will be present throughout the whole recruitment process. Here are two examples of well-known companies EVP:

"We're dedicated to building an inclusive culture where employees can do their best work. ... Giving HubSpotters the freedom and flexibility to create their own work-life balance builds trust in our company, but it's also just the right thing to do." – **Hubspot**

*"If you're looking for a place that **values** your curiosity, passion, and desire to learn, if you're seeking colleagues who are big thinkers eager to take on fresh challenges as a team, then you're a future Googler."-* **Google**

One of the main reasons for leaving a job after a short tenure is that the vision that was sold to the applicant during the interview didn't translate into reality; in other words, their EVP has not been met.

Even if you are not ready to formalize this process yet (or perhaps you are a manager or HR manager who is having trouble influencing senior management to implement such a strategy) it is still essential for a good recruitment process that you at least understand why someone would want to work for your organization. Additionally, you should be able to clearly articulate these reasons.

How your employer brand can attract HPTs

Forward thinking, up to date employers recognize that the hiring of a new person is a two-way process and that the first step towards attracting high performers is to ensure that the impression of the company they receive is consistent, from that first communication (whether it is a direct application or through a recruiter) right through to when they join your company. With a strong EVP in place you have the foundation to develop and promote your employer brand. Over the next few pages we are going to explore ways in you can develop your employer brand to aid the attraction of high performance talent.

Your Employees

Your employees are your best asset. You need genuine brand ambassadors who seek opportunities to engage online with the general public and who have face to face contact at conferences and seminars. The Employer brand already exists in the people that already make up your teams. Talk to them, gather information and find out what they are saying, what they like/dislike about the organization. Use this information to send out the right message both internally and externally to develop brand awareness. When any new potential employee carries out their research on your company what are they going to discover that is going to make them want the opportunity even more?

Company Website

Using the internet and social media is an excellent way to develop and promote your employer brand.

Starting with your own company website, when was the last time this was reviewed from an applicant's perspective? Take yourself on their journey, they are interested in working for your company so their first stop is to visit your website. How easy is it to navigate to the careers pages and once there what information does it share?

A good careers page will inform the applicants of the following:

- What the company can offer them and the benefits of working for the company. (Employee value proposition).

- Describe the culture of the company allowing them to get a feel of what it might be like to work for your organization.

- Clearly list the current vacancies and how to apply.

- What to do if a vacancy isn't listed, but they would like to submit a speculative application.

- Information about diversity and inclusion.

- Company values.

- Environmental responsibility.

Some companies even include a 360 degree video tour of the work environment. This provides potential applicants with a great overview of what it might be like to work for the company.

LinkedIn

LinkedIn can be used to showcase who you are as an organization and used as an extension of your website. If you are a company who is hiring regularly then it is advisable to set up a 'jobs' page. You want to create an environment that shows who you are as an employer. You can do this through putting out messages on successes, achievements, expansion and growth plans etc. Positive messages put out on LinkedIn help to develop your employer brand but you must ensure this is done consistently. As with the website content it can be damaging to your brand if the last items posted are from a number of months ago.

Other social media platforms
Other platforms that can be used include Facebook, Instagram and Twitter. Entering into this type of process shouldn't be taken lightly and it will require you to have someone who can continually update and maintain these sites whilst keeping the message on brand but also fresh and engaging. One of the benefits of LinkedIn, Facebook and Instagram is the ability to target your company to certain demographics. If you are, say, seeking to hire lawyers as is the case in Muldowney Legal, then identifying targeted groups to post your message out to will mean you are going directly to the place where these individuals "hang out" online.

You can create a culture of brand advocacy by encouraging all employees to actively engage with social media through the provision of interesting content, plus the continual cascading of consistent information up and down the organization increases the likelihood of being constantly 'on message'. Company policies on how information should be shared externally, where to access the right information and what information is acceptable to share should all be communicated from their 1st day. When introducing new schemes to current employees gain their input and ideas from the beginning. Encouraging employee involvement gives them a sense of ownership and enables them to see the benefits and for everyone to reap the rewards of everyone being on the same page.

Hashtags

The use of hashtags is highly advisable if you wish to reach a wider audience. Any news article, image or message that is put out on a social media site, ensure you have used appropriate hashtags. It is certainly worth conducting your own research online to find out what are the most active hashtags in your particular sector. There are many different websites that can aid this for example Hashtags.org, tweetreach.com and ritetage.com. And don't forget to check out the hashtags that are currently 'trending' on Twitter and using those in any relevant tweets you are sending out.

Measuring the effectiveness of Employer Branding

A significant amount of time and cost is involved in developing and maintaining an employer brand. It would be a disaster if the hard work and effort put in was not actually making an impact or worse still having a negative effect. Measuring the effectiveness of your employer branding schemes is essential and can be done in a variety of ways:

1. Higher quality of applications

    It is usual for the number of candidate applications to be tracked when people apply for vacancies with a company and how they heard about the opportunity. Each candidate can then be tracked to see how they perform throughout the recruitment process. As new employer branding schemes and initiatives are introduced you should ensure that a tracking system is in place to monitor the quality of applicants coming through that scheme, the percentage of applicants that go through to each interview stage and how many hires are made through this method. You might even go as far as tracking longevity of those hires.

2. Reduction in time per hire

    Do you know your current time to hire from when a job vacancy first becomes live? How effective is your employer branding initiatives in speeding up the response and bringing new hires on more quickly?

3. Reduction in cost per hire

    What was the source of the applicant and the associated cost. For example if a specific campaign has been launched to attract a certain type of candidate then have in place a monitoring system to manage the responses and the cost to run the scheme and monitor the outcome.

4. Number of relevant applications

    It is not unusual to have a large volume of applications and find that a high percentage of those are just not relevant to the role. A lot of time can be spent filtering through applications that are just not suitable. It is essential that you have thought about how you are going to target the right audience.

5. Engagement and productivity after appointment

    Monitor how quickly new hires settle in to their post, ensuring once they are hired the internal employer branding schemes are incorporated as part of their induction. Regular formal and informal reviews can be carried out to assess how engaged a new hire is and review the impact their work in having on the team/division/ company.

6. Reduction in number of recruitment consultant partners

    The very best companies have extremely strong relationships with one or two preferred suppliers who service the senior vacancies and then no more than three recruitment partners to work on a more contingent basis.

    By limiting the number of recruitment consultants you work with means you are able to develop a relationship where the recruiter could almost be employed by you because they know the company so well they become part of your employer brand. They are one of your champions and know how to sell an opportunity to a candidate and communicate why they should work for you.

Examples

Let us look at two of our example companies and how they might apply principles of employer branding to their very different companies:

Muldowney Law clearly has a need to address its employer brand. It has staff turnover challenges and is finding its ability to attract and retain the right type of talent limiting its growth plans.

Megan Doyle has therefore implemented an employee engagement survey as part of the post-merger integration plan. The survey will be looking at what people like about working for the firm and what ideas they have to improve employee satisfaction. She will also evaluate feedback she has had from exit interviews that show evidence as to why individuals have felt disengaged from the general company mission.

In conjunction with the firm's Marketing Director, she is engaging a marketing research consultancy to work with local recruitment consultancies to evaluate what is most important to potential applicants of the type the firm wishes to hire. Using this information they will put together a marketing campaign that is ostensibly aimed at the clients customer base, but is also values orientated with a message that emphasizes the investments that the firm makes in the development of its people. This will be driven hard in the local Dublin area.

Her objective is to completely reverse Muldowney Law's somewhat negative perception in the market place and build the firm's reputation as an employer of choice.

SGT initially had limited resources and their management team has very little experience on how to build teams. They were unknown as a brand, so they had no previous employer brand either positive or negative.

Their strategy for hiring the talent they require was to hire as many developers, engineers and project managers through local networks. This had its limitations, but it is a sensible very early stage strategy for an early stage company.

As the founders saw it, they had three distinct advantages with respect to their employer brand; one, they believe they have a clearly defined culture (this needed to be further developed and honed as previously discussed), two, they are rapidly growing with good financial backing, and three, they are getting extensive publicity in the local area due to winning innovation prizes etc. They ensured that articles that were appearing in local press, professional magazines and online articles emphasize the opportunities that the company offers.

They therefore successfully built an effective EVP around SGT being a fun vibrant place to work with great prospects, and used all the opportunities they could to promote the fact that they are growing rapidly and hire bright clever people to come and join in on their success and growth. It is an EVP that is very appealing for their sector and resulted in a steady flow of applications from recently graduated software engineers, which made up a substantial part of their requirement in their early phase of growth.

Exercise Five: What makes you a stand out employer?

Even if you already have an established company EVP, write down the key reasons why you think an individual should work for your company and why people like working there. Perhaps ask the people that report to you and who work for the company across multiple departments. This way you will get a broader and more accurate view.

Assessment 5 - Why would someone want to work for you & your company?

Using the information gathered in Exercise Five, now write below which of the key points you think really make your company stand out from other employers. (If you can't think of any reasons, why are you staying there?!)

1. _____

2. _____

3. _____

4. _____

What you discover from carrying out this exercise should be fed back into your hiring process. Good companies send out an application pack which includes the Job Description and Person Specification but also information about the company, the culture, what the company is like to work for.

It is imperative that everyone involved in the process is aligned. How is the person coming across on the phone when they call the applicant to book the interview, how are the applicants greeted as they enter the building for their interview? If you are using a recruiter how well do they know your business and the message they should be getting across. You have to take a responsibility for this, and make sure that you are briefing the recruiter effectively.

They should be acting as an extension of your organization.

At every stage through the hiring process you should be pushing out the employer brand message about who your organization is and why someone would want to work for you, whether you eventually hire them or not.

Your actions from this chapter:

- Review and assess your employer brand. What message are you putting out both internally and externally? Where can improvements be made?

- Assess and review your social media presence, what information if going out, are you receiving interaction and are you putting out the right messages consistently?

- Find out what is (or what would) make you are an employer of choice and reasons to shout about it.

- Make sure from the top down you are working towards the same hiring strategy and all promoting the same message to ensure best practice and applicant experience.

- Why developing an EVP is important for candidate and employee retention.

Let's do a quick recap of what we have learnt so far:

1. We have reviewed the economics of getting it right and wrong – high performers v low performers.

2. We have given you a recruitment process to follow and why structure is key to successful hiring.

3. Explained what 'great looks like' and why company culture is important when attracting and hiring HPTs.

4. Discussed the high performance indicators and how these can be used when identifying HPTs.

5. Why investing in your employer brand is going to attract a better quality of applicant.

The next stage of the process (see page 43 Successful Recruitment Process flowchart) is to look at understanding your business and determining your actual business wants and needs.

Chapter 5
Business Needs Analysis

Understanding your organizations wants and needs
First and foremost you need to have a full understanding on the future plans for your organization. Before deciding on the types of people you want to hire you need to establish the wants and needs of the business. Once you have this understanding you should be able to map where the gaps are in your current team. So when considering the type of person you wish to hire, review your business plans and figure out "wants and needs" and then identify the type of profile that would allow you to achieve this. Essentially this type of approach is about gaining a proper understanding of what the overall objective of a job function is and what contribution that job makes to the overall business objectives.

Once you have a full plan in place on what the business will look like and the direction it is heading in, you will then be able to work out the key elements and job functions you require in order to meet those objectives and milestones.

Understanding the key elements for a role

- **Technical or product/service specific requirement**

   What is the most important essential skill set? For example, does the Software Developer that is required by SGT need to be skilled in 3-D graphics development, or is this really just a "nice-to-have"? Does the German Sales Specialist for Acme Medical need to have capital equipment sales experience? Does the new lawyer required to specialize in life science sector need previous experience in this sector?

   Sometimes it seems that hiring companies limit their hiring pool and consider possibly non-essential "technical" skills to the exclusion of everything else, without really asking themselves, "is this genuinely essential?"

   Once you have considered what is essential as a knowledge base, you need to decide what skill set is required to do this role and how you are going to evaluate a potential candidate's current understanding or their ability to acquire that knowledge.

- **Interactions**

   What are the other functions that this person will interact with? Who are the people internal and external to the organization, and what are their characteristics? What skills and attributes does a person doing this role need to have in order to deal with these interactions?

- **Processes followed**
  What are the processes that this individual will be developing, following or implementing? E.g. Are they required to use ERP systems or CRM tools?

- **Location**
  Where does the person need to be based geographically? Where would their optimum base be? Do they need to be near an office, or based from home? How often will they need to attend the office? How much time are they likely to spend travelling and be away from home? Is the role international in its scope?

- **Key Performance Indicators**
  How is the person measured? What is their productivity target likely to be? What metrics are used and what skills if any are needed for self-assessment of performance? How would you expect someone to achieve high levels of performance? (You would expect HPT to exceed expectations, to bring with them ideas and methods that have been proven to work in the past, and to be innovative and a creative.)

- **Reward systems and salary**
  Where are you compared with the market in terms of the compensation and benefits you offer to your employees? Do you have any data? How attractive is your bonus scheme or Long Term Incentive Plan if you

have one? If you wish to attract top performers you will need to be in the upper quartile, but you do not necessarily have to be the top payer if other elements of your offering make your proposition attractive.

Remember that you should not base a salary package on what you have paid someone in the past but on what the market value currently is.

- **Hiring from the competition?**
You may be tempted to hire a person that has worked for a competitor. Many people love the idea of taking a competitive hire. It is a 'double whammy' – you hire someone who is already maybe dealing with your customers, or who knows how a particular product type is engineered or developed, and you frustrate your main competitor in the process!

It cannot be denied that there are some cases where this approach works quite well and, if you are looking for quick market penetration, or to perhaps hire someone that needs less training it can be a very seductive strategy. However in many cases it simply results in you hiring someone who may have management issues, has a lack of loyalty, and who is probably not performing well. So what is the likelihood that they will perform better for you? Unless this is a promotion for them, why are they moving? It is essential that you understand their motivations. Our recommendation is that, if you are 'competitive hiring', proceed with caution.

NB: With competitive hires you may also have to consider including a 'non-compete' clause within the candidate's contract.

- **Changing conditions**
  Is the market that you operate in changing? The most likely answer to this is yes. We are currently in a period of exponential change in many sectors. Globalization, market consolidation and political upheaval, and changing requirements from candidates mean that what may have been a necessary skill set 5 years ago may not be applicable today.

Learning from previous successes and mistakes

Now you have fully understood the business wants and needs you can delve into past recruiting successes and failures. Study the attributes of your most successful hires, your high performers, your low performers and your failed hires (normally your short tenures).

Are there any patterns?

Megan Doyle has identified a number. Unsurprisingly, their high performers demonstrate most, if not all the High Performance Indicators. They all have stable job records prior to coming to work with Muldowney Law, and their previous jobs showed strong evidence of achievement. All but one, live in fairly close proximity to the office.

When looking at low performers, it is almost an exact mirror image. They have very few of the High Performance Indicators and there is nearly always a lack of stability in their previous job records.

With failed hires there appear to be two types. Some actually appear to have stable job records, with a few who have actually been at one company for a long time. Looking at feedback from exit interviews it appears that they did have the right profile, but a failure in the onboarding process has resulted in their EVP (page 68/69) not being met.

The second group of failed hires often have unstable job records and a complete lack of evidence of achievement on their CVs, and also suggestions at exit interview of a lack of alignment with respect to their EVP and cultural and behavioral values.

This type of evaluation is invaluable if you have had previous problems in your recruiting processes. It is even helpful if your processes have been reasonably without disaster, as it is an opportunity for process improvement that increases the chances of hiring and retaining more HPTs.

Summarizing the skills you need

Once you know what the key elements to your specific role are, you now need to understand what you want from a functional perspective.

The next few pages offer a detailed example of how this may look. This should aid the shaping of your own needs analysis.

Example:

Profile Description

Acme Medical – Sales Specialist – Northern Germany

A new position, part of Acme's strategic expansion into Europe following their recent acquisition of a hoist business. A functional skills assessment for the role indicates the following:

The product range
Is largely made up of capital sale items, with a limited number of consumables. Additionally, the German market favors rental models for these types of products. Compared to many medical products it is not a highly technical sale from a product perspective and service engineers largely cover this aspect.

Skill need: Ability to sell capital equipment. Should ideally have knowledge of rental or finance schemes in order to enable this type of sale.

The customer type
Is mainly defined as a professional purchaser. Many are parts of group purchasing organizations. Additional key influencers will be hospital managers and professional end-users.

Skill need: Ability to sell to professional purchasers. High negotiating and solution-selling capabilities preferred.

The sales process
It typically takes a minimum of six months from the initial sales enquiry. Some leads are provided by the company but as this is a new territory it will require someone who is able to generate new leads themselves.

Skill need: Ability to generate leads: a 'hunter' mentality /capability.

The territory
Northern Germany.

Skill need: Ability to use good sales-effectiveness skills to manage a large territory. Ideally, should have experience using a good Customer Relationship Management (CRM) software. Is able to travel and to speak both German and English fluently.

Key Performance Indicators

Are based upon various criteria that must be entered into the CRM system and which provide a guide to the additional resources required as the territory grows.

Skill need: Ability to be goal- and target-oriented, combined with good organizational skills.

The reward system/salary

As the company is NOT a market leader from a size perspective, it is recognized that, in order to compete for top talent, the base salary will be in the top quartile for the sector. Additionally, the commission scheme will be designed to be the most rewarding scheme in the sector for high performers, with a system that is simple to understand.

Competitive hires

Will only be considered if it can be demonstrated that they have a clear and understandable reason for considering the role. Their scores at interview will need to be at least equal to those of non-competitive candidates, according to most measures, in order to be considered.

Assessment six: Essential Skills

Carry out an essential skills assessment for all roles within your organization. It is far better to do this in advance of need rather than only when the need arises. To put into simple terms an essential qualification or skill set should be required if the person would be unable to carry out the job without it.

The software developers in SGT are being hired to carry out a specific job function which requires them to have a qualification in software programming related to 3D imaging. The person they seek to hire must already have this experience for the project objectives and deadlines to be met. Therefore this is an Essential Skill. If we compare this to a desirable qualification or skill, then these are the 'good to have' skills but not compulsory. So in this example if the person had experience of geological exploration of the deep sea-bed then this would be a "good to have" but without it they would still be able to carry out the job and learn this skill whilst in post. It is normally expected that the candidate will learn any 'desirable' skills or qualifications later as part of their job role.

Using the example above as a guide, complete Exercise six from this you should be able to form the functional aspects of the job description and an applicant specification. The former describes the job to the applicant, while the latter describes the skills attributes and behaviors you will require the applicant to possess. It therefore provides a template for anyone involved in the recruitment process.

Exercise Six - Essential and desirable skills need analysis

Company overview

Technical Capabilities

Interactions

Process capability

Outline the location
Outline the KPIs/Objectives (that is, what are the KPIs/Objectives and how would you expect someone to achieve them?)
Salary and Benefits (Describe the salary and benefits that you can offer. What is the market value for this type of position?)
Competitive Hire – (What are the advantages and disadvantages of a competitive hire?)

Writing an effective job description

Writing a job description (JD) is a good opportunity for the hiring manager to consider the role and what they wish to achieve from the new hire. Even if a JD already exists for someone that has left, it is sensible to review it and decide whether it still meets the needs of the present-day business.

As mentioned previously, many sectors are experiencing rapid change, so a JD from a year or two ago may or may not be pertinent to your requirements today or the future plans for that job function. A new hire might not only be the opportunity to look for HPTs to raise the standard of your team, it may also be the opportunity to look for a successor to a manager, or maybe someone with additional or completely new skills that were not required previously.

Most JDs are often dry and uninspiring: a dull shopping list of responsibilities, mainly designed for internal consumption. They may also include acronyms and jargon that might be meaningless to a candidate. If you wish to compete for the best talent, you should ensure that your JDs are anything but dull! After all, you will be expecting the candidate to have a good CV, so why shouldn't a candidate expect a good company to have a well-thought-through JD?

Furthermore, a well-structured JD makes:

- An excellent briefing template for internal and external stakeholders such as other interviewers and recruiters.
- An essential tool for gaining the interest of candidates, the importance of which cannot be overstated.
- A key document for structuring the interview and recruitment process.
- A key tool for aiding the decision to hire.

The best JDs for recruitment purposes are externally focused. They should contain the following:

- Company overview (size, history, number of employees, locations etc.).
- Business overview (products, market position, growth etc.).
- Location requirements (and the flexibility of these requirements).
- Roles and responsibilities (which should sound interesting, not dull!)
- Profile requirements (stating what is essential and what is desirable).

Additionally, they should:

- Be legally compliant for all geographies covered.
- Have a diversity policy statement and be written in a language that is inclusive.

- Avoid using company jargon or acronyms.

Like a CV or resume is normally the first impression you will have of a candidate, the job description is the first impression the candidate will have of the company and job position. If a candidate receives a misleading message on a JD it may be enough for them to disengage.

Example job description and application specification

Acme Medical Inc.

Job Title: Territory Manager for Northern Germany

Location: Germany: Northern Territory. Includes Bremen, Hamburg, Mecklenburg-Vorpommern, Lower Saxony, and Schleswig-Holstein.

The role may be carried out from any part of the territory defined above, but preference is for the Territory Manager to be based within 50 to 100km of Hamburg.

Function: Field sales.

Our company: Acme Medical Inc. is a $261M US manufacturer of hospital beds and patient-handling equipment that is highly respected for market leading quality. Founded in 1982 in St Paul, Minneapolis, Acme Medical employs just over 1000 people worldwide. With a direct operation in Germany, we are entering a major phase of growth and expansion that will further strengthen our European presence. We have been rated by our employees as 'a great company to work for' in recent global surveys conducted by the industry magazine Medical Devices Now and have a personal development program and career progression opportunities that have been described by the same magazine as 'outstanding'. Acme Medical is proud of its high performance culture, offering excellent growth potential for its employees.

Purpose: Reporting to the DACH Regional Director, the Territory Manager for Northern Germany will primarily be responsible for driving new business across the territory, and developing professional relationships with key opinion leaders, group purchasing organizations (GPOs), hospitals, and private clinics.

Responsibilities:

- To visit customers and/or potential customers of Acme Medical on a regular and planned basis to promote products and services in order to achieve monthly, quarterly and yearly sales targets, as agreed with the DACH Regional Director.

- To evaluate and develop leads in order to provide short-, medium-, and long-term business pipelines.

- To review monthly objectives with the Regional Director.

- To use modern solutions-based selling techniques in order to best respond to customer requirements.

- To keep the customer relationship management system up to date and use analytics to optimize territory management.

- To develop business relationships with GPOs,

purchasing departments, hospital management and hospital staff.

- To acquire a full knowledge of finance and rental schemes and adapt them to customer requirements.

- To engage in our company training program and thereby acquire and maintain an Acme five-star-rated technical product knowledge.

- To provide ongoing technical training and support to customers.

- To attend exhibitions, meetings and conferences (as required) in order to promote Acme Medical services and products.

- Work with the DACH Product Manager to ensure full integration of marketing tools into selling process.

Applicant specification

[NB: part of this may be included on documentation you send to candidates, either as a separate document or as 'requirements' and therefore part of the job description]:

- Has an exemplary record of stable employment [NB: this can be defined but should not reference years of experience as this would be seen as discriminatory in some countries] and exudes a professional and positive attitude.

- Has the ability to sell capital equipment and ideally has knowledge of rental or finance schemes that will enable this type of sale.

- Has the ability to sell to professional purchasers. A high negotiating and solution-selling capability is preferable.
- Must have a 'hunter' mentality/capability; that is, the ability to generate leads and close deals.
- Should be goal- and target-oriented, combined with good organizational skills.
- Should have the ability to use good sales-effectiveness skills in order to manage a large territory.
- Ideally, should have experience using a good CRM tool.

Acme Medical is proud of its reputation as an equal opportunities employer and embraces diversity. We do not discriminate on the grounds of gender (including pregnancy and gender identity), race, age, faith, disability, national origin, political affiliation, sexual orientation, marital status, disability, age, parental status, or military service.

[NB: it is sensible to get local legal advice on equal opportunities and diversity statements.]

Note to recruiters [NB: this would not be shared on a job description given to candidates]: People from competitors will only be considered if it can be demonstrated that they have a clear and understandable reason for considering the role. Their scores at interview will need to be at least equal to non-competitive candidates according to most measures for them to be considered. They will need to declare whether they have restrictive covenants in their contract that would in any way restrict their ability to work for Acme Medical.

Salary: Between €xxxxxx, and €xxxxxx. In addition, we offer a 30% bonus and company car (to the value of €xxx per month). Salary and benefits are not to be shared with applicants.

Exercise Seven – Create a Job Description and Person Specification

Using the information in this chapter and your own information detailed in exercise/assessment six (page 92/93); create a job description and person specification for a job role you plan to hire. Ensure you incorporate the elements discussed in the book thus far.

Highlight the key high performance indicator traits you are looking for and detail information on your D&I policy.

This document is a selling tool, until the applicant attends an interview this information will give them the first insight into what the company is like and what the job entails. It therefore needs to be exciting, enticing and provide enough information that the applicant can attend an interview and perform at their best.

In this chapter we have looked at:

- Fully understanding the wants and needs of the organizations to achieve the business objectives which could be to grow, diversify, open a new office etc. to establish what job functions need to be recruited and how many.

- How to learn from previous hiring successes and failures.

- Being able to identify the knowledge needed to fulfill the different job functions.

- How to break down the skills required to carry out a job function and if they are essential or desirable.

- How to create a job description that is going to sell the opportunity to an applicant and how to create a person specification that details the necessary skills.

Chapter 6
Candidate generation methods

Choosing your 'candidate generator' method: is it up to the job?

Following the preparation of 'what good looks like', the job description and application specification, you are now in a position to start generating candidates in a number of different ways. The methods you use to generate candidates are fundamental to success. When many line managers complain that the recruitment system is broken, i.e. the lack of choice, or the complete lack of quality candidates, it might be for a number of reasons, but the most common cause is that the candidate generation method has failed.

Some methods of candidate generation may appear to be

relatively inexpensive, while some may appear to be the opposite. The numbers discussed previously underline the fact that any process you may take that radically increases your chances of hiring an HPT is extremely economic. Therefore any additional cost that is incurred in the pursuit of such individuals needs to be seen in that context.

As mentioned earlier, the best way to reduce the cost of recruitment is to recruit more efficiently. Short-term cheap will almost certainly mean long-term expensive.

There is no risk-free way to recruit, any more than there is a risk-free way to do most important things in life. What we can do is apply a robust structure to the process and look for ways to manage parts of the process that enhance our chances of success.

If you want to acquire top-quality people you will need a reliable way of providing a decent number of suitable-quality applicants to subsequently choose from. Part of the key to success when hiring HPTs is to understand that skills are more important than experience, and that attitude is more important than anything else.

Having a large number of candidates to choose from does not automatically guarantee quality by any measure. Twenty CVs will do you no good if they are all of very poor quality. As a client of ours recently discussed with us, the danger of his line managers having a lot of people to interview is that they feel they have to make a selection at the end of it, because even a mediocre candidate looks good if they are surrounded by applicants that are even poorer. The hard truth is that many companies that find themselves in candidate-driven markets are falling into the position of hiring poor-quality people due to the poor choices offered to them. Many HR/talent acquisition teams and bargain-basement recruitment consultants really are taking an 'any candidate will do' approach. This is often because their candidate generating model is not targeted or varied enough.

The following are the potential sources to generate candidates from:

- Personal recommendation of the hiring manager
- Advertising and online job boards
- Social media sites
- Use of hashtags
- A company referral scheme
- Internal Talent Acquisition team
- Contingency recruitment companies
- A retained search-consultancy partner
- Temporary, contract or interim recruitment
- Online CV database

It makes sense to ask what market penetration your approach is getting. That is; is there a reasonable chance that you will generate a level of interest that will provide you with genuine choice, within which will be the HPT or perhaps a choice of top performers?

If you are just relying on recommendations and an advert on social media, sending a few messages out and ending up with only a few candidates that approximately fit your job brief we would respectfully suggest that you are not taking this hire too seriously!

For most hires it makes sense to have a mix of these methods, either simultaneously or sequentially. It should be carefully considered in order to ensure that one method is not counter-productive against another. For example, if you have invested in a retained search method, it does not make much sense to also be using other methods such as advertising simultaneously or a contingency recruiter, unless that is through the retained search partner.

Let us therefore look at the relative merits of each approach in generality.

Personal recommendation of hiring manager

Many hires are made on this basis. The attractive aspect is that the person is already a "known quality", very often perhaps having worked for the hiring manager previously. The hiring manager will therefore have a much better understanding of the person's capabilities than any amount of interviewing or assessment can manage.

The downside to this approach is that considerable amount of bias then enters the process. Is this person really the best person out there? Well possibly, but what processes have been put in place to really assess that thoroughly? There is also the question of diversity. Is this person another clone of the hiring manager, hired for convenience or because they will be compliant and non- challenging? A number of these situations have a common sense aspect to them. If you are in charge of a number of teams and one individual always favors hiring this way, possibly to the exclusion of other methods it is worth assessing the quality and diversity of those teams. As a general rule, if a person is fortunate enough to be able to hire some of their team this way, that is a positive, if it is most then probably not so much!

Advertising

Advertising is a very popular method of recruiting, particularly for junior to mid-level roles and almost all job advertising is now exclusively online (although you still do see some jobs advertised in the local and national newspapers). Advertising a job effectively is something of an art and a differently worded advert can produce greatly varied results.

There are numerous job boards and places to advertise. It is sensible to look at those that address your market best. Do your research on this. Ask the job board for the number of candidates registered on their site within your particular sector who have the job title you are looking for, and how many of those candidates have been active in the last 6 months. The better ones have a vast amount of analytical information that they can share with you. Compare two or three job boards on the size of the potential candidate pool, life time of the job advert and how they may be able to assist you in getting the most out of the advert. If this is your first time posting a job then some sites will be able to advise on how to optimize your job advert to get the best results. This is also an opportunity to test out different job boards, quite often you will be able to negotiate a month's trial if it is likely that you will be posting jobs regularly and having that job board as a partner.

When it comes to writing the advert, a good job advert speaks to the individual, and should be skills and benefit orientated, and addresses what is in it for the candidate. It should be an extension of your company brand positioning, and its objective should be to get shared.

For example:

Territory Manager- Northern Germany – Medical Devices

Our company, Acme Medical Inc. is a $261M US manufacturer of hospital beds and patient-handling equipment that is highly respected for market leading quality. Founded in 1982 in St Paul, Minneapolis, Acme Medical employs just over 1000 people worldwide. With a direct operation in Germany, we are entering a major phase of growth and expansion that will further strengthen our European presence. We have been rated by our employees as 'a great company to work for' in recent global surveys conducted by the industry magazine Medical Devices Now and have a personal development program and career progression opportunities that have been described by the same magazine as 'outstanding'. Acme Medical is proud of its high performance culture, offering excellent growth potential for its employees.

(note this is exactly the same as on the job description – some adverts may need this to be précised.)

As Territory Manager for our North Germany territory, you will have a highly professional and positive attitude combined with an outstanding record of achievement. You will have experience in the field of selling capital equipment to professional purchasers and healthcare professionals in Northern Germany. You have a "hunter" mentality/capability and are highly goal and target orientated with excellent organizational skills enabling you to be able to maximize on the market leading benefits package and growth potential that this opportunity presents.

To apply for this position please contact (email address etc.)

Acme Medical is proud of its reputation as an equal opportunities employer and embraces diversity.

We do not discriminate on the grounds of gender (including pregnancy and gender identity), race, age, faith, disability, national origin, political affiliation, sexual orientation, marital status, disability, age, parental status, or military service.

Advertising has significant limitations. First and foremost is the fact that the candidate pool is mainly made up of "active" job seekers. This is good in some senses, but it also means that you are competing with all the other employers. You will also need to manage the application response if you are doing this direct and not through a partner. If you have a very large response and fail to respond to people, even those that are completely inappropriate (and there will probably be lots of these) you will damage your employer brand. On the positive side, it is a good method to compliment other methods.

Wherever you choose to advertise your job, be it on a jobsite, your own website or somewhere else always test the usability and end user experience. What does the advert look like from their perspective? A survey carried out in 2019 showed that 79% of job seekers used their smartphone for job search. When planning and designing your job advertising campaign ensure you have thought through the journey the end user will go on. You have a limited amount of time to capture and hold their attention and the last thing they want to be doing is scrolling through numerous pages of a job advert. They don't want to be having to zoom in on the text because it is not been optimized and they do not want to have to "jump through hoops" to apply. There should be a clear call to action. And is always sensible to have a 'share' button as they may just know someone who would be perfect for the job.

Social media

As we have mentioned in the chapter on Employer Branding, social media is an outstanding opportunity for companies to position themselves and their job opportunities to attract a wider candidate pool.

A social media site such as LinkedIn is considered to be a highly professional 'business' networking forum where like-minded people can connect to create opportunities.

Companies can have a jobs page within their company page where they can post jobs out to the network. Individuals can follow your company/job page and set up notifications to be alerted when new jobs are posted.

Employees on LinkedIn can share a link to the job posting on the company website from their individual page which is then seen by their network. It should be encouraged that other members of the company who are on LinkedIn also share the post to broaden the reach.

LinkedIn has developed some great functionality for employers to use this platform as a way to generate candidates. They have different levels of service depending on your annual hiring needs. For light touch recruitment you can opt for the pay as you go option which allows you to post a single job as and when the need arises. If you are more likely to be an occasional hirer then Recruiter Lite may be a better solution. This allows you to access 3rd degree profiles and offers a number of InMail's per month to approach potential candidates.

For high volume recruiting then Recruiter may be a preferred option which gives you access to the whole LinkedIn network and a large number of InMail's to use monthly to approach candidates.

The functionally offered by LinkedIn is evolving all the time and something you should be aware of. You can find yourself working in a certain way and one day that functionality has been removed and you have to change your approach. Whichever method you choose they all come with an administrative responsibility. If, like with online job boards you put an advert out, you need to have someone assigned to managing, filtering and responding to all the applications. From the statistics LinkedIn reports then you would be expecting to see a good return on the investment.

With Recruiter or Recruiter Lite, although notifications can be set up to inform you of profiles that match your requirement, you will need someone to assess and approach any suitable matches. These systems require a large time investment to research, approach and track candidates and neither are 'cheap' solutions so to ensure you are getting the most for your money this task needs to fully form part of someone's job function. If you are trying to use these systems alongside your 'day job' then it is recommended you find alternative candidate generation methods otherwise you will be investing in a system that you will not be getting the most out of and will be very costly as a result. On the plus side, if used well, this system has the potential to unearth "passive" candidates that may not necessarily be looking for a job but would consider listening to opportunities and exploring further.

It is worth noting not every person who has an account is an active user (although the numbers are still huge!) According to a Kinsta report in 2020, LinkedIn had over 575 million user with just under half actively using their account on a monthly basis. It is also noted that 40% of those who have a Linkedin account are active users on a daily basis. If you are just relying on LinkedIn searches to find candidates you are limiting your pool and the potential to reach HPT. These people it could be argued are likely to be less active on social media as they are likely to be doing other things with their time.

In comparison Facebook reported in the first quarter of 2020 they had 2.99 billion active monthly users across their social media apps including Facebook, WhatsApp, Instagram and Messenger and of those 2.36 billion were active daily users. Facebook has some excellent functionality to attract talent. Many companies set up a company page where they showcase what's happening in the company and highlight the company culture and strengthen the employer brand. Facebook offers the options to post jobs ads and this can be done on a relatively small budget and to a very targeted audience, your aim here is to make your advert enticing, what do you know about the audience you are trying to attract that is going to engage their attention and encourage them to click to find out more information. As mentioned before you ideally want to encourage your employees to share your posts and jobs to maximize the reach of your content.

When we are considering the social media platform you use to attract High Performance Talent we need to choose a platform that your demographic are using actively. There is little point running a campaign on LinkedIn if the target audience are most active and engaged in Instagram. It is therefore essential that you carry out your research and possibly even run some pilots campaigns. Remember, it is not what you think is important but what the candidates you are trying to attract thinks is important; they are the ultimate decision maker. We should strongly highlight that while you must be mindful of not being age discriminatory, there are certain platforms that are more likely to be utilized by certain job types, or levels of seniority.

It will be beneficial to encourage employees to link their profiles to a company page and to "like", follow and share on sites such as Facebook, Instagram or LinkedIn and ensure they are getting regular content reminding them why they work for a great company, thereby also encouraging them to "spread the word" to friends, family and acquaintances.

Hashtags

As mentioned earlier hashtags can be very effective when used in conjunction with adverts, and it is suggested that you should use a mix of small, medium and large hashtags to maximize your reach. A quick bit of research online will quickly show the best hashtags to use for your job opportunity. There will be the general ones for example, #jobsearch #hiring #jobseeker, but you may wish to target your job post. If, say, the job is for software developers, as is the case with SGT, then you would be wise to carry out some research to identify which hashtags are being used to reach that specific target audience. Don't guess and use something like #softwaredeveloperjobs as this may have very limited activity and very few people may actually see it. Hashtags will always be evolving in popularity and so it cannot be stressed enough to carry out your research here.

Company referral schemes

Company referral schemes can be very effective. Individuals who have experience in other companies will almost certainly know other good people. If they are happy themselves they will be able to be an advocate and persuade people whom they have previously worked with the merits of joining your organization. Most companies incentivize this with a sum of money payable when the person starts.

Internal Talent Acquisition (TA) team

Talent acquisition function and remit varies between companies. In some organizations they are largely administrative, coordinating activities with external partners, and in others they are more pro-active, sourcing candidates through various means.

In many cases companies have set up Talent Acquisition teams to address the "broken recruitment" challenge, and in others their objective is to save money through the reduction in the need for external recruiters. If the latter is the primary objective, leaders of organizations should be careful of false economy as demonstrated in the earlier chapter on the economics of hiring. It is our opinion that a good TA team can be highly effective if properly trained and resourced. Conversely a badly trained and resourced TA team, that simply uses one or two simplistic methods to find people can be extremely damaging, causing poor hires with the resultant economic and reputational damage to your company. While a good TA team can help fix the broken recruitment problem, a bad TA team can exacerbate the issue. Our recommendation is that you should never hire someone for TA that you would not hire for a strategically important senior commercial position. This person will be selling your brand to the outside world. If their salary is low, or they have had 5 jobs in the last 5 years there is probably a reason for that!

We have recommended to clients that they may want to consider bringing up high potentials through a secondment to TA, where they can learn invaluable experience on hiring that they will then be able to use in their capacity as a line manager. Fundamentally, if you have, or are considering having a TA team, it should be made up of the highest caliber individuals you can imagine. These are appointments where an "anyone will do" approach should never apply.

A good TA team will look at all aspects of recruiting including, cost, time to hire, effectiveness of recruiting methods and be able to produce solid reliable statistics on hiring into the organization, for example, tracking number of applications per role, the source of the applications, conversion to first interview etc.

Contingency recruitment companies

The majority of recruitment firms operate what is known as a "contingency model". What this means is that they present candidates for particular role and if you hire a candidate presented you pay a fee based on a percentage of salary or package, and if you hire no one then you pay nothing. Candidates are normally taken from a database of already known individuals, and therefore the candidates tend to be those that are actively looking for a job, and maybe considering a number of employers.

This model has a number of apparent benefits to employers, particularly for higher volume, lower salary staff. It appears to be relatively risk free, with fees only being paid when absolutely necessary.

Unfortunately, contingency recruiting has what could be best described as something of a varied reputation.

The firms range in capability and reputation from outstanding to terrible, from exceptional professionals to out and out cowboys! Using the latter can be highly damaging to your carefully crafted employer brand, and such recruitment companies have considerable responsibility for the widely held belief that recruitment is broken. Employers that continue to engage with these organizations (usually because they are cheap) share that responsibility!

How can one therefore find the outstanding recruiters and discard those that we do not want our brand associated with?

The best recruiters, whether they are contingency or retained (the latter discussed below) are discerning. Like all good professionals they are looking for a good working relationship with clients. They are unlikely to be interested in being used as a "plan B" or safety net for companies that are mainly interested in only using them if they are unable to find candidates for themselves or who wish to bench mark against an internal applicant with no real intention of actually considering the external applicant seriously for the job role.

To fully understand this it is first best to understand how the contingency recruitment model works. Contingency recruiters work on the assumption that only a certain percentage of vacancies they manage will be filled by them. Some positions will be filled by other recruiters, some by the company directly and some will be cancelled. This means that for a large percentage of the roles they nominally represent they will receive no payment for the work they carry out. Sometimes this work will be significant, sometimes less so. Either way, when you hire someone through a contingency recruiter you will, to a large extent be paying for all those "clients" that did not pay anything. Contingency recruiters will therefore, unsurprisingly, prioritize work that is most likely to bring a result, and this is one of the primary reasons potential hiring managers get frustrated when their own role does not receive the attention they believe it deserves. In reality, contingency recruiting is very mercenary. They know that many, if not most of their clients have no loyalty to them. If they are operating in a "candidate-led" market they will be looking to push the best candidates out to a number of clients, thereby knowing they are maximizing the opportunity of getting that candidate placed.

Now that we understand how the system works, this will inform us on how to get the best from them.

Essentially, if we are going to achieve a good outcome, we need to choose a recruiter that is appropriately qualified and networked to do the job, and is sufficiently motivated to prioritize your position over those of your competitors for those people.

The following questions will help you choose the right one:

Question 1 - Are you a specialist in my sector?

Question 2 - What are you company values and how do they align with who we are and what we are about?

Question 3 - How do you like to work with your clients and foster long term relationships?

Question 4 - What methods do you use to attract candidates (check they are using the most up to date methodologies)?

Question 5 - How long will it take to generate appropriate candidates?

Question 6 - How do you qualify candidates suitability?

Questions 7 - What methods of candidate communications do you use?

Questions 8 - What are you success rates?

Questions 9 - What are your fees and what adjustment would you give for an exclusive arrangement? (if they are cheap - avoid them – see below!)

Questions 10 - What is your rebate structure, and how often is it used?

Question 11 - What questions do you have for me (the client)?

Question 12 - Why should we use your recruitment company compared to others?

Avoid companies that are cheap. In a candidate-led market there is no reason for anyone to be cheap, whether they are a contingency recruiter or a retained one, unless, of course, they are no good! If they do not have the confidence to be charging in the upper quartile for their services they are most likely chancers and are hoping to get lucky. You wouldn't go to a cheap lawyer to undertake a mergers and acquisition process, nor an inexperienced doctor if you had a serious illness, so why would you rely on a cheap recruiter for your most important hires?

Having chosen a firm that you think in principle meets your needs, discuss with them the job brief, preferably face to face if you have not dealt with them before. If they do not demonstrate the specialist knowledge they have claimed this will become apparent in the discussion. If this proves to be the case you may wish to reevaluate, and certainly do not offer exclusivity. Exclusivity is a major incentive to a contingency recruiter who is any good. Two or three weeks will give them an opportunity to steal a march on their competition, and they should make full use of this.

When they have taken the vacancy brief, ask them to ring you back the following day and sell the role to you as if you were a candidate. This will give you an idea of their capability to sell your role in a competitive environment.

You should avoid simultaneously competing between your internal TA team and external recruiters. If an external recruiter becomes aware that this is happening they will quickly deprioritize your role, and will seriously damage your relationship with the recruiter, and may even cause confusion in the market place with a negative impact on your employer brand. Ideally you should have your TA team working roles that are not with external recruiters and allow the external recruiters to do their job. If your TA team has already worked a role they should inform the recruiter who they have already considered and rejected.

The best way to put your vacancies at the top of the priority list with your recruiter if you:

- Set aside time at the start of the process to fully brief your recruiter.

- Provide a job description and person specification.

- Provide timely and appropriate CV and interview feedback.

- Set targets for first and second interview dates.

- Provide regular communication throughout the process.

- Pay a fee level that demonstrates you are serious about finding high performance talent.

A retained search-consultancy partner

There are many positions, or projects that justify a retained consultancy approach. This should be regarded as the "gold standard" of candidate generating. If it does not prove to be so, it may be that you have chosen the wrong partner.

Again, cheapness is nearly always an indicator of poor service. Expensiveness is not necessarily always the converse though! It is fair to say that one should be wary of companies that are predominantly contingency offering retained search solutions. The models are entirely different and their priorities not the same. A good retained search consultant expects to fill ALL vacancies that they are assigned. You are essentially buying their time to reach an end point. This is in contrast to the contingency model described earlier.

Additionally you are not looking to find candidates from a database. You are asking the search partner to use their knowledge, network and know-how to target a market and approach people, many of who are not currently looking for a role, but maybe persuaded if they can be contacted. The best researchers in such firms are relentless in their pursuit of people, and will transparently report back on their responses. You are looking to systematically target the best talent; that is, the people who are most likely to have the skills you need. These will be the type of candidates who are probably not on anyone's database.

Some recruiters (particularly contingency recruiters) will claim they have 'done a search', whilst unable to provide evidence of their activity. Where have they searched? Is it just their database, or a few approaches on LinkedIn? The best recruitment companies are transparent in their process and can demonstrate how they will go about the recruitment process in detail should you ask for it. A professional retained search consultancy will ensure that you are being advised and supported throughout the process and will know how to properly assess talent.

As with choosing a contingency recruiter, there are a number of questions you should consider asking before hiring a retained search consultancy:

Question 1 - What are you company values and how do they align with who we are and what we are about?

Question 2 - How long have you been doing retained search, and what knowledge/evidence can you provide of similar searches/projects to the requirements we have?

Question 3 - How do you like to work with your clients?

Question 4 - What research methods do you use to identify candidates?

Question 5 - How do you approach candidates and how would you sell our opportunity/company to them?

Questions 6 - How do you assess candidates?

Questions 7 - How do you communicate with candidates and keep them interested?

Questions 8 - How do you report on the progress of the search?

Questions 9 - How do you structure your search fee?

Question 10 - What is your candidate replacement or rebate policy?

Question 11 - What is your off-limits policy? (which companies will you be unable to approach on our behalf)

Question 12 - Why should we use your firm for this project?

Temporary or contract/interim recruitment

The focus of this book is really orientated toward permanent staff. However, there are many occasions where temporary or interim staff offer an attractive solution. If you are growing rapidly and need a quick solution, or maybe you need to fill a gap while you go through the rigors of a search, temporary or interim staff maybe a very good solution.

A lot of the same rules apply. One strong tip is to take staff that appear "over-qualified" for the role. This is particularly the case with interim managers. They will need to be "parachuted in" and will need to be able to understand the business team or project needs quickly based on their previous experience. Sometimes it may provide an opportunity to move someone from temporary to full-time. This may not be possible with someone who is a "career interim" – they enjoy the flexibility being an interim brings, but in some cases this may work well, as the period they are working on the temporary contract provides evidence of how well they fit in and can do the tasks required.

Whether you use a 'talent acquisition' team, a temp recruiter, contingency recruiter or a retained search partner, it is highly important that they are very well-briefed, highly professional and extremely motivated to focus on your specific roles.

Looking again at SGT, it is quite likely that their candidate generator model is not up to it. If they have only filled 40% of the roles they have open it needs to be assessed what the reason for this is.

Part of it may be alignment between the founders, resulting in them missing good people, or a lack of prioritizing by them resulting in processes taking too long.

Most likely, though, when they are 60% down it is due to their candidate generator model. They are simply not getting the choice in the first place.

This was probably because of their preference to hire through their own networks to save money. This is foolish and quite clearly a false economy as their inability to hire fast enough is risking missing their milestones. In the introduction it was clear that their funding round was oversubscribed, so they could have budgeted for this, and they should have. Had they had a person on the team that drafted their business plan that understood the hiring challenge they were going to have they would have set aside a greater budget. They have now realized that they will need to reallocate budget from elsewhere to afford the recruitment consultancy services they need to plug the gap. They have now identified which profiles they can continue to hire through their own networks, which they can access via social media and advertising and which they need to get recruitment consultants to help them with.

We have shared some important aspects to candidate generation through this chapter, the main areas for consideration are:

- Fully understanding the different types of candidate generation methods and their pros and cons.

- Understanding that a combination of candidate generators are going to ensure that you access high potential candidates, not just "any candidate will do".

- The importance that your chosen methods for candidate attraction do not work against each other as this is hugely counter-productive.

- The vital importance of properly briefing your search partners, TA, and recruiters on the role and the type of person you are looking for.

- It is essential that you know and understand your audience. You chances of successful engagement are only going to work if you are catching their attention in the first place and using the right candidate generation method.

- Images and videos are a powerful way to capture the interest of the people you are targeting and it is proven to increase engagement.

Chapter 7
Short Listing, Interview and Assessment
Getting your management team(s) fit for purpose

You might have the best products, a great company image and amazing customers and follow a great recruitment process, but if your management team are all working to their own agenda and not company focused you will not attract or retain high performers. High performers and high potentials are more sensitive to who their line manager is. Most such people need someone they can respect, trust and listen to, and want to know that they can expect the same in return. It is often said that people don't leave companies, they leave managers.

By extension, people don't turn down companies that interview them, they turn down interviewers. If you are implementing an high performer acquisition strategy, you will need to ensure that your line managers and/or colleagues involved in the interviewing process have absolutely bought into the program and, most likely, they should show the same high performance indicators (as discussed in chapter 3 page 53/54) that you expect from the people that will work for them. If your interview process involves three senior managers and they are giving off mixed messages this is of great concern and could be very off putting to the HPT. Additionally you will need to make sure that they follow the strategies in this book in order to stand a chance of reaping the reward of attracting the very best people.

It is surprising how many hiring managers are expected to build teams but have never been given any formal training on how to recruit and hire. We believe this aspect is another key driver in the recruitment is broken narrative; most interviewers are just not very good at understanding their own needs and then how to transpose those needs into efficient interviewing.

As mentioned above, it is essential that hiring managers have "buy in" to the process but it can all go badly wrong if they do not have the first clue on how to actually conduct an interview and identify key indicators that would differentiate a 'good to average' candidate from a high performer.

Hiring Managers have a critical job and just because they have the title 'hiring manager' it does not necessarily mean they have the skill set or ability to hire others. They have normally been promoted for some other reason, like technical expertise, or leadership potential for example.

Companies should provide interviewers with the tools they need to conduct a thorough and effective recruitment process. They need to be able to see this function as a critical part of their role, not just something they have to do amongst all the other things they are juggling. It should be firmly in their top 3 priorities. If it is not a priority, it needs to be asked why are they in the job?

There are so many elements to getting hiring right and some of the areas hiring managers should be given training on include:

- As the earlier chapter suggests, understanding the economic impact of hiring decisions.

- Their role and the roles of others during the recruitment process.

- How to write an effective job description (see page 95).

- Understanding employment laws and their implications.

- How to prepare for interview, including assessment of CVs and applications.

- How to prepare and ask the right questions.

- How to evaluate genuine high performers and high potentials.

- Offer Negotiation

- Successful on-boarding

Reading this book will be a good starting point for hiring managers, and additionally we recommend specific interview and selection training, either on a suitable training course delivered in house, externally or via online training portals.

When our example company SGT first received its most recent round of funding it knew that in order to deliver the growth promised to investors it needed to hire a significant number of new technical staff and experienced project managers in the subsequent 3 years. This second phase of recruiting was far more intense than the earlier days of their development, and using the methods they had used before (mainly networking and an almost accidental building of a good employer brand) failed to produce the volumes and quality of the people they now needed. Not only were the people they now needed much harder to attract than they had forecast, they also discovered that the recruiting process was a considerable distraction from their other work – work that they were more disposed to prioritize. There was also a lack of alignment between the founders as to what type of people should be hired first for the new phase. Fundamentally, they did not have a management team that was suitable to deliver one of their most mission critical aspects of the company's growth plan; i.e. the hire of the new team.

It was not until 12 months into the hiring project that they realized something needed to be changed. They had hired only 40% of the people that they should have done by that point and it was badly affecting their ability to hit their milestones.

Following significant pressure from their board, they agreed to bring in an experienced HR Director who had extensive experience of managing the processes required to achieve staffing growth at the pace required. The new HR Director, Vince Price, recognized that urgent corrective action was required, which included training of the three founders and the newly appointed Project Heads on how to select and interview high performance staff.

CV reading and interpretation

You've written your JD, briefed the recruiter, and the HR team has received a shortlist of resume/CVs, together with reports as to why the candidates meet the functional requirements and the HPT criteria. If you are working with a well-briefed retained search consultant, you might be expecting to interview all of the candidates they have sent, or maybe five out of seven, or something to that order.

If you have done your own advertising, or are using multiple contingency agencies you might have a very large number of CVs to filter.

If you are filtering, we recommend you adopt a 'rule-in' rather than a 'rule-out' policy, particularly for the first assessment. What this means is that it is better to look at reasons why you should include an applicant, rather than reasons why you should exclude them.

As an old colleague of ours would say, 'remember that you are not hiring a professional CV writer'.

In other words, just because a CV isn't perfect doesn't necessarily mean that the person behind it won't be good.

This may particularly be the case in this scenario as you are looking for HPTs' attitudinal aspects – these are difficult to accurately interpret from a CV.

You should have a copy of the JD and applicant specification easily to hand. If you wish to be as 'scientific' as possible, it might be sensible to adopt a scoring system, awarding points for various skills, experience, job stability, etc.

Such an approach may also be helpful for best practice in relation to the avoidance of discrimination; if it can be demonstrated that someone has been rejected on the basis of a non-discriminatory points system you will be able to demonstrate to them, if required, that they have not been wrongfully discriminated against.

Check key functional needs, e.g.:

- Location - ability to work the territory, sensible daily commute or able to relocate.

- Qualifications – is a specific qualification or further degree (MSc, PhD) a requirement or a preference? In many environments qualifications may be considered desirable but non-essential. Also, if a qualification is listed it is good practice to state "or equivalent".

Specifics, e.g.:

- Specific experience

- Specific customer type

- Geographical remit

NB: It is really important to ask yourself when conducting this exercise whether there are alternatives to your specific needs.

Check your key wants (essential and desirables), e.g.:

- Demonstrations of achievement

- Customer networks

- Languages

Having removed any candidate CVs that are obviously not aligned with the specification through the first assessment, it is then sensible to try to see what is behind the written page on the remainder.

Recall how one of Megan Doyle's key objectives was to significantly improve the quality of the people they were hiring, and through her analysis was able to identify key correlations between underperformers and characteristics that were observable on CVs. For example, she noticed that underperformers, and short-tenure hires that had been dismissed, generally had very poor job stability. She decided that if the person had x number of jobs in a given time period, this would be enough to be a red flag.

This may not be a reason to not include that person in your shortlist of applicants, but it will certainly be an area to explore at interview. Do they have good reasons for leaving each position, how confident are they in obtaining references from any of those employers etc.? If you are using a recruiter then you would expect to have received this information when the CV has been presented to you. If that was also combined with at least two other areas of concern, such as a lack of achievement focus it would mean the person would probably not be called forward for interview.

If your filtering has left you with none or only one or two candidates, this may be due to one of the following reasons:

- Your expectations are too high.

- Your candidate generation methodology is sub-optimal.

- Your contingency recruiter has either been poorly briefed, or they are not fit for purpose!

- (After a thorough market analysis) your retained partner has established that this candidate profile is in extremely short supply.

Assuming you have a decent group of remaining CVs, check that the dates and months of employment are consistent, and assure yourself of the time they have worked in each role or company. If you are unsure, then it can be beneficial to arrange a short telephone interview as part of the process or, if you used a recruiter, call them for further clarification.

If you have used a recruitment partner or a talent acquisition team as your main candidate-generation method, they should have thoroughly interviewed and screened candidates in order to assess their functional capability and their HPT indicators. Your internal interview team will need to reaffirm these to some extent and carry out their own due diligence, but nine times out of ten the candidates should be of high quality and should be taken through to interview.

Interviewing: preparation and interview skills

The interview process should be enjoyable and rewarding for all those involved. Preparation for it is a highly important exercise, as time spent preparing well could mean you find the person who is going to change the direction of your business, boost sales or efficiency, or even directly or indirectly lead to your promotion. A poor choice resulting from a 'slap-dash' approach may have the reverse consequences.

You need to know what your process for interview is going to be. Know who is going to be involved, how many interviews will be required and when they will be. In other words: work to a plan (see page 43 for the recruitment process flow diagram). In our opinion, not all interviews need to be face to face, particularly initial interviews. In many situations a video facility such as Skype, Zoom or FaceTime can be used, and is much more convenient for interviewer and interviewee. There are considerable time savings to be made which might result in gaining an advantage over our competitors. Provided the video quality is good, these types of interview are greatly superior to a phone interview, which in the light of the availability of such technology should be the interview method of last resort. It is not to say that phone interviews should never be used, just that they are not nearly as effective at creating the ideal communication ambiance.

Whether you are interviewing face to face or via other media, it is correct to say that in order to interview candidates well, you need to properly prepare – a top candidate will have prepared themselves, and you should do the same. Read all the candidate- or recruiter-supplied documentation you have been given (CV, covering letter and the email with which the CV was sent) and review the company for whom the candidate currently works.

Use this information along with your needs and wants to

compile any specific questions for each individual candidate. These should supplement a list of standard questions that you ask all candidates in order to allow you to benchmark each candidate. However, do ensure that any variation from your standard questions passes your inclusivity requirements and are not in any way discriminatory.

Some people like to use competency-based questions. Our opinion is that, if overused, such questions may seem cold and impersonal. If you wish to employ people that are cold and impersonal then maybe that is fine, but perhaps you prefer to make the person believe that they are in conversation with a human!

The fashion for these questions grew out of the supportable belief that examples of past performance will best illustrate future capability, and that it is also possible to ask a list of questions that each candidate can equally be asked. It is, however, more than possible to achieve both objectives without asking every question by starting with 'Give me an example of when you have ….?'

If you choose this interview method then decide what competencies and skills are most important and how you can align them with your HPT requirements. Then, compile some questions that will prompt discussion around key areas. These questions should therefore include function based questions, performance based questions and HPT behavior indicator questions, and they should follow the profile that is defined in the Profile Description (see chapter 5 page 89).

If we therefore look at the Profile Description prepared by Acme Medical (see page 89) for their Sales Specialist Northern Germany we can see how they prepared the questions listed below. Their interview process is split into three stages; the first with European General Manager, Lena Rollinger, and then preferred candidates have a Skype interview with Tim Brooker the VPHR and a final interview again with Lena Rollinger.

They have therefore prepared enough questions to make the interview process progressive, and not repeating the same questions, **see examples below:**

Function based questions

- What accounts do you work with and in what geographical area?

- What experience do you have of capital equipment selling?

- What do you consider to be the principle challenges and opportunities with selling rental schemes?

- On a scale of 1 to 10, and assuming that we may test you against this later in the process, how would you rate your technical knowledge of the products you are currently selling/would be selling for us?

- How important do you believe technical knowledge to be to the sales process?

- What is your opinion of CRM systems as a tool for assisting sales performance?

- What methods do you use to prioritize your time?

- What defines a 'key account' for you?

- What does 'sales effectiveness' mean to you?

Performance based questions

- What market share do you believe you have in your territory, compared to your nearest competitor, and how does that compare to your company generally?

- What growth have you had in your territory, and how does that compare with colleagues and/or market averages for your product?

- Describe an account or customer that you took from low performance to high performance and what you did to achieve that.

- Please describe your greatest achievement in the last five years.

- How have you performed to target in the last 'x' years, and how has that compared to your colleagues?

- Please can you detail for me any competitions or awards you have won, or successes that you have had, over the past five years.

HPT behavior differentiator questions

- Do you consider yourself competitive and, if so, how competitive do you think you are?
- What do you consider to be the key characteristics for great salespeople?
- How would your colleagues describe your sales ability?
- Please describe an example where you used an innovative solution that resulted in a significant sales win.
- Do you believe 'the customer is always right'?
- What is 'solutions selling'?
- Please describe an example of where you have overcome a strong objection from a customer that resulted in sales.
- Please describe an example of where you have provided a solution for a client/customer that was one they had not considered prior to discussing it with you?
- What training have you had on sales?

- Who is/are your favorite author(s) for sales, negotiating, or general business?
- What training have you recently undertaken to develop yourself?
- What is your main motivation for success in sales?
- Can you please describe for me how you would sell a new product to a customer who has not used it previously?
- What do you do that ensures you close business deals with customers?
- What does 'ethical selling' mean to you?
- To be successful in this role requires resilience. What makes you a resilient person?
- How would you convince us that you are someone who can persuade our customers to buy our products?
- What do you think you would want to achieve in your first 12 months and how would you go about it?

Acme Medical are unlikely to use all these questions. There simply will not be time to use them all. They will therefore need to prioritize which ones they think will be best and then apply these consistently across the candidate selection.

Note: In recent years there has been a fashion for using what some call "differentiator" or "brainteaser" questions. We prefer to refer to them as "crazy" or "pointless", and we strongly recommend that they should not be used. Examples are "Explain a chair to an alien?" or "if you were an animal what would you be?"

Advocates of these types of questions believe that they show how "smart" a person is and their ability to think laterally. It does neither of these things. In fact a recent study by *Applied Psychology Today* demonstrated that a liking for these types of questions merely indicated "dark personality traits" such as narcissism and sadism of those that use them! The important message from all this is that if you want to attract the very best people it really is not a good thing to make them think you are a sadist.

Aggressive or "smart-Alec" interviewing may well be a turnoff to the very people you want to hire. On top of this, as we now know that the people that ask these questions are likely to be seen as narcissists or sadists, is this great image for a hiring company's employer brand?

Our advice is, avoid these type of questions. They achieve nothing!

Exercise Eight – Role specific Interview questions

Using your essential and desirable skills need analysis essential needs and skills analysis from Exercise 6 (page 93 and the HPT indicators exercise (page 60/61) prepare the following for a role that you are likely to be recruiting for:

- 5 to 10 Function Based Questions
- 5 to 10 Performance based Questions
- 5 to 10 HPT Behavior Differentiator Questions

The questions you are forming here are the questions that you should ask every applicant that you are interviewing for a particular role. This ensures a consistency in your approach and a fair and unbiased process. This approach allows all interviewers to review the applicants objectively. You are likely to have some specific questions for each candidate related to their individual skills, experience and achievements.

General interview skills: the 'first' interview

The first interview is often not really the first interview! If you have a recruitment partner the candidate should already have been interviewed against the basic criteria. So, for our purposes, we will define the first interview as the first time the candidate meets the potential employer.

Before the candidate has even arrived to meet with you there are some crucially important aspects to ensuring the candidate arrives prepared and feeling confident. It should be obvious that they will have been informed of the date, time and location but what else do they need to know in advance?

We strongly recommend informing the candidate of the following:

- Who they are meeting which should include their name(s), job title and even a link to a website if you include employee profiles or a link to their LinkedIn account.

- Advice on travel to the office if it is to be a face to face meeting. Is there parking or should they arrive by public transport?

- What, if any, information should they bring with them to the interview?

- Make sure they have received the job description and person specification.

- Who should they contact in the event of an emergency?

Providing extra information in advance of the interview will allow them to prepare and ensure they perform at their best at interview. Also, you will be able to discover if they have in fact read the information provided and whether they have they prepared insightful questions as a result of the reading and the research they have done. The candidate has an opportunity here to demonstrate how serious they are about the candidature from the outset.

When you first meet the candidate, take every opportunity to give them the chance to relax, to get to know you, to shine, and to impress you. Do not expect them to answer every question perfectly to your expectations. You are looking to hire an individual, not a robotic clone. You will get much better results from being friendly than being adversarial. The approach on The Apprentice might make amusing TV, but it is a terrible way to really find out about someone. By all means ask tough demanding questions during an interview, but the bullying tone of the out-of-date 'pressure' school of interviewing may well have the best candidates getting up and walking out. HPTs will do this to interviewers they don't like.

Fundamentally you should be treating this person with respect, as a customer of your brand, and you should remember that this person could have a significant impact on your business and your career. Leave them with a negative impression and you may be simultaneously missing out on a great candidate and damaging your company brand.

How to structure the interview

The interviewer should open up, set the scene, explain the role, challenges, and opportunity. You may even decide to say that one of the objectives of the process is to find High Performance Talent and to describe the process upon which they are embarking. Avoid starting with the question 'tell me what you know about [my company]', because they may answer 'tell me what you know about me'!

If you have more than one person in the interview process decide in advance how you are going to make the interview progressive and not all cover off the same questions. Ideally you would assign each interviewer a specific role so that all evidence of interview performance can be fed back and reviewed together. For example at Muldowny Legal, HR interviews specifically look at cultural alignment, team working, time management etc. Whereas the senior partner deep dives into specific experience and achievements related to the role they applying for.

We once asked one client of ours what it was that he did when interviewing, as everyone that came back from interview with him wanted to work for him. It transpired that he spent the first five to ten minutes of the interview telling the candidate about his own background and why his company was great to work for. He was a genuinely likeable individual and this approach put the candidate at ease and made them enthuse more about the role. It essentially meant that he had the pick of the best candidates, as they all wanted to work for him.

The fundamental idea that many interviewers and companies lose sight of is that the interview is a two-way street!

You hope that you may have a choice of candidates, but in a candidate-driven market the better candidates will always have a choice of options too. Just because you are a hiring manager representing an employer does not make you a superior being! Treating candidates in a supercilious or arrogant manner is likely to see the best people repelled from your organization. You probably know of colleagues that do this. Encourage them to stop. They are not achieving anything, whilst damaging your company brand.

For your first interview, no matter the type of interview that is taking place (face to face, video or telephone) you should follow the following structure:

- Introduction – tell them about yourself and the company and opportunity. Sell yourself to the candidate before you expect them to sell themselves to you.

- Review work history, background and reasons for changing jobs. Be careful not to use all your allotted time on this.

- Questions (this will occupy most of the time of the total interview).

- Achievements and accomplishments.

- Motivations for a career/job change.

- Compensation – establish their current compensation and what their requirements are.

- Interests – these are often neglected in interviews and, if discussed, can enable you to see more of the 'real' person.

- Process – explain what the next stages are (even if you are repeating what was said in the introduction).

- Does the candidate have any questions?
- Close the interview.
- Subsequent Assessment.

After your first interviews you will need to decide who is going to proceed to the next round. An objective scoring system is best for this purpose. You are not deciding at this stage which candidate you are going to hire; rather, you are asking yourself (and colleagues) who the candidates are that meet your criteria.

Note that we don't say the 'best candidates'. If you simply just choose the best of this round there is a danger that you do not adhere to your objective. What if none of them are good enough to meet your expectations? It could be that your expectations are unrealistic but, if you have followed the previous recommendations, that is unlikely.

If you do not have the right caliber of candidates then it might be that you have specified wrongly or that your candidate-generating system is not fit for purpose. It is also worth noting that sometimes personality comes into play, a person may appear to be appropriate superficially but their fit to the company culture may not align and their suitability to fit into the current team may not marry up. Assuming that this is not the case, then you will need to consider who fits the criteria. It may be two candidates, it may be three. If you are fortunate and you think it is greater than three, you should only now choose the best. Ideally, you should not proceed to the next stage with more than three candidates.

Second or subsequent Interviews

Further interviews should always seek to be 'progressive' and logical; in other words, they need to move the process forwards and they should have a purpose.

They should not, as previously mentioned, repeat the same questions as the first. They may ask a similar question to the first in order to gain a different angle, or they may take the approach of seeking further clarification relating to something that has been discussed before.

A list of progressive questions that should be asked at second interview should be agreed between the interview team. It is recommended that one person from the first round joins the second interview panel as this allows that interviewer to compare performance between the two stages.

Additional methods of assessment

If you are to have a very robust process of selection, you need more than simply a round of interviews to assess candidates, particularly if you really want to assess the HPT indicators.

The most obvious additional method is to use personality and aptitude tests. You can use these to test against high performance indicators; specifically, you can test the candidates' aptitude for those aspects of the role that you consider to be the most important. If you agree with our assessment that HPTs generally show high IQ and EQ, these factors can also be tested.

Some people like to use these tools later in the process; say, after the first stage and only for candidates that have reached the final stage. Some of the questions in the second interview may be derived from a combination of these results and the previous lines of questioning to further progress the process. Most industrial psychologists agree that such tests should only be used as supporting evidence, and perhaps as guides to additional questions. They should not be used in a 'rule-in-rule-out' manner.

If you are considering multiple hires you may want to consider an assessment center. A well-run assessment center can provide a very effective appraisal of someone's ability, approach to team work and possible cultural fit. The chief advantage of an assessment center is that they test what a person can do, not what they know. Many candidates participating in an assessment center tend to see the process as a good test of their ability to do the job for which they are being considered; often, they enjoy the experience. The biggest challenge with assessment center as a concept is that they will only really work if you have enough participants who are all available on the same day!

Such an approach could be very appropriate for SGT. They are hiring a lot of people, and with high growth rates comes pressure on integration. It would be very valuable to see how well these individuals worked in a team setting.

An alternative to an assessment center may be to see how candidates behave in a more relaxed environment. This might involve giving them a tour of the office or factory. Some people may even favor a social setting, such as an evening out. One client of ours likes this as she says that it is interesting to see how a person relates to others such as waiting staff – is the candidate arrogant or aloof and, if so, does this fit with the company culture and values?

One of the biggest challenges if you are assessing some people is that many know how to give the impression of being HPTs when they are not. They may charm their way through interview processes and say what they know the interviewer wants to hear. These people are very good at convincing interviewers who rely on gut instinct and who do not use robust systems to check claims. If you feel that the way the person comes across does not align with your evidence, never ignore the evidence, however friendly and pleasing their personality appears to be.

At all stages through the process ensure the candidate experience is exceptional!

It is not difficult to find evidence online of job seekers who think recruitment is broken. The experience offered to many applicants for jobs the world over is not acceptable; there is a lack of basic applicant care and post-assessment feedback by some HR and talent acquisition departments, hiring companies and recruiters. This is not only impolite, it may also be highly damaging to the brand of both the hiring company and anyone else associated with the process. The expectation that a relatively inexperienced recruitment consultant, talent acquisition or HR person should be able to deal with a senior or highly technical appointment is unfair on that staff member and on the applicant. It also looks highly unprofessional from an employer branding perspective.

One of our long-standing clients is one of the most effective proponents of a high standard of applicant care. What do they do that many others ought to? Here are some examples:

- They treat their applicants as customers

    They accept that they can't hire everyone that applies to work for them, but they realize that it is very bad PR if a person does not have a good experience! Their sector is a 'small world'. People talk, and many will be networking either with customers or with other people they may wish to employ in the future. They want people to share a positive message about their overall experience.

- They partner with professional recruitment partners

    They choose to work only with highly professional recruitment companies that fully understand their company and its values, so that the very best candidates have a 'seamless' experience throughout the process.

- They ensure that anyone coming forward for interview is properly briefed

    A well-briefed person is most likely to perform at their best and is most likely to buy into the company. In the first five minutes of any interview, the company and opportunity are 'sold' to the candidate, making them understand that the company is always serious about their candidature. Sure, they ask challenging and probing questions of the candidate; however, the candidate is always left with the impression that this is done in a respectful manner, thereby ensuring that a match is made that will suit both the company and the candidate. This way, even if a candidate is rejected for the role, the candidate is left with a positive impression of the company's professionalism.

- They offer a transparent recruitment and interview process

    They do not think it is acceptable or desirable to attempt to be clever with the candidate or to try to catch them out with trick questions during the interview.

    It is essential that the message you are putting out is consistent and that it continually reflects who you are as a company. This is the first image of your company that is presented to the candidate, so they must like what they see and hear if they have agreed to attend the interview.

The next step is to ensure that your brand and image are consistently projected to the candidate, all the way through the interview process. Make sure that you have the right people interviewing for the appropriate level of appointment. Give timely feedback, both good or bad.

Whatever the outcome, ensure that the candidate walks away saying really good things about you and your company.

- They give balanced, well-thought–out and prompt feedback

There are, after all, only three decisions: yes, no, or wait! If it is the first, then surely you want that candidate to know immediately so that you can maintain momentum? Time is of the essence when recruiting high-quality people! If it is the second, then you should also let them know immediately, as why make them wait? Be fair and reasonable as they have invested their time as well. If it is the last alternative, you should be able to give them reasons as to why there is no immediate decision.

Reference Checking

The final and a highly important aspect of the assessment is reference checking. This will normally take place after interviews and often it is left to the very final stage. If at all possible, it is useful to have references for any candidates that are coming back for the final stage. This may be two or three individuals. In our experience, HPTs are proud of their reputation. They will nearly always have several people you can talk to, though some may be reluctant to allow you to talk to them until the offer stage, for understandable reasons.

If a candidate is in any way hesitant about showing documentary evidence or giving references from previous line managers and colleagues you should be deeply skeptical. The most important aspect about reference checking is the candidate's willingness to provide references, followed by the level of equivocation in the reference itself. Candidates that are reluctant to give references should be treated with caution, those that are unable to find anyone who can speak on their behalf should be avoided. Never do unofficial 'backdoor' reference checks without the candidate's consent. These are not only unethical, they are also illegal in many jurisdictions, most notably in Europe as they contravene data protection rights (i.e. the General Data Protection Regulations (GDPR). Infringing these rights often entitles the individual to compensation; additionally, the company who has committed the infringement may incur substantial fines.

Ideally your references should be checked verbally over phone or Skype.

The following questions generally work for most roles:

1. How long have you known the person?

2. Have they reported directly to you? When/how long?

3. How would you describe her/him generally?

4. How was she/he in performance terms. i.e. meeting agreed objectives?

5. How was she/he perceived by peers?

6. What are her/his key strengths and areas for development?

7. If you had the opportunity, would you employ her/him again?

8. Any further general comments?

A large amount of information has been covered in this chapter, to recap:

- Assess the capability of the hiring team and arrange relevant training

- How to read and interpret CV against your hiring requirements

- Know you interview process in advance; who will be interviewing, when, type and desired outcomes.

- Examples of interview questions that you can use and an exercise to help you prepare your own.

- Things to consider at each interview stage for both the interviewers and the interviewee.

- Why candidate experience is essential to your hiring success

- Example questions to ask when taking a reference on a potential hire

Chapter 8

Hiring Success and Beyond

Pulling it all together: comparing candidates – who should 'win'?

Your aim at the end of the second round of interviews is to decide on who you wish to hire. Using your JD, your needs and wants, the applicant specification (including the HPT Indicators), your interview notes, the answers to your various questions and the thoughts of your colleagues, you will now need to decide who is, ultimately, the final preferred candidate or candidates.

If it is difficult to differentiate between the candidates, you may need to revisit your scoring system. You may wish to weight certain criteria more strongly than others. There are a number of the things you can score against:

- First and foremost: do they meet the high performance criteria that you are looking for?

Additionally:

- Does their reason for leaving and what you are offering connect?
- Will you be able to offer the opportunity they seek?

- Will they fit into the team?
- Do you get on with them?
- Are they bringing new skills to the team and to the business?
- Have they future developmental potential?
- Do they require training and, if so, do you have the time and resources?
- Are you focusing on attitude, skills, or experience? As mentioned previously, too many hiring companies are far too fixated on experience, often to the detriment of skills and attitude. Someone may have had ten years' experience of, say, software development, but what did they learn during this time? Clearly, for any professional role, a level of experience is necessary to gain the skills required.

However, someone with the right attitude and opportunity may gain those skills at a far greater rate than someone else. Demanding 10 years' experience of 'x' may not only be indirectly discriminatory in some jurisdictions (in that it is discriminating against younger candidates) it is also a very poor indicator of skills. Remember also that you may now be looking at a different profile to what you have looked at in the past. If you take the example of Muldowney Law, Megan Doyle has identified that the profiles hired in the past are no longer fit for purpose, and there are areas identified which should be focused on.

The offer

When you get to the stage of making an offer, the best place to start is by putting yourself in the candidate's shoes when that offer is made. What would your reaction be? If you are using a recruiter it is sensible to get them to position the financial details of the offer with the candidate 'in principle', prior to the candidate being offered the position formally. The recruiter's discussion should be something along the lines of:

"I believe it is looking promising that an offer will result from this process.

While I cannot guarantee that an offer will be extended, can I confirm what your expectations are?"

Should the expectations be out of alignment at all, the recruiter should say:

"OK, are you therefore saying that if an offer of XYZ was extended you would walk away, or would you still wish to consider the position?"

Whatever the finer points of the negotiation are, do remember that, where you have a choice of candidates, the best candidate for your role is nearly always the one that is the most enthused about taking it.

In order to mitigate the risk of losing your preferred candidate there are a number of things that can be established during and after the interview process or supported by a recruiter.

These include:

- Providing timely and sensible feedback during the process and always informing of timescales and next steps.

- Current salary and benefits package. Where possible be 100% clear what they are earning. If they state a total package per annum how does that actually breakdown into salary bonus and allowance. When discussing bonuses find out how much they actually earned not what they 'could' earn. Do they have private health, pension percentage, home working allowance, car or car allowance etc. It has been known that an employers preferred candidate has turned down a job offer because a company car was part of the package and they were already leasing one that was under contract and there was no work around. We have also seen employers offering a sign on bonus to candidates to secure them and overcome say lost bonus from their current employer to get them to start sooner. In circumstances like this working with a professional intermediary can be extremely beneficial in the negotiation phase.

- Salary expectations based on their current package, what is being offered against the role and market value.

- Be clear on their motivations for changing jobs, a warning bell should be going off if you get a sense it is purely money motivated. In this instance there is a risk the candidate is using this process to angle a counter offer from their current employer.

- Are there any contractual restrictions such as a non-compete clause that you would need to take into account should you hire them?

- What is their notice period and does that fit with your timescales for hiring. Are you prepared to wait if it is 3 months? It is also highly advisable to engage with the candidate during their notice period. We have heard of candidates who have received no contact from their new employer during their notice period and on their first day they did not show up. When investigated they were unimpressed by the lack of engagement and had found a different job.

Post-hire quality process

One of the principal reasons for new hires failing and only lasting short periods is as a result of inadequate onboarding and a lack of subsequent monitoring and mentoring of the person. Research suggests that about 70% of employees are more likely to stay with a company for three years if they have experienced great onboarding when starting a new job.

Skipping a company induction and poor onboarding is putting the new employee at risk of failure and this has a follow on impact for the company. If a company provides an onboarding experience that educates new-starters on the company's brand and their individual part to play in the culture, it ensures that employees feel that they are part of something bigger, a future. If you have gone to the trouble of sourcing an HPT, it is a tragedy to allow them to become disenchanted and to then either underperform or leave. Simple steps can radically reduce the likelihood of this happening.

Firstly, make sure everyone who interacts with the individual is part of the plan, particularly the line manager. It should be decided who is taking ownership of the onboarding – a member of HR or the line manager (though in our opinion it should be the line manager).

The following should be in place:

- A written plan for onboarding, with a checklist to ensure that all aspects are covered.

- A welcome pack that includes the company handbook and policies.

- A timetable for their induction showing them when they have training, meeting team members, tour etc.

- A briefing on company culture and introduced to colleagues, and made to feel as welcome as possible.

- Issued with any handover documentation, company literature or reading materials and anything they need available on day one.

- Provided with a clear indication as to when they will be able to start working autonomously.

- Agree with line manager when regular one-to-ones in their early weeks will take place and they should always be available on their first day.

- If they have a workstation in the office, ensure it is smart and ready, equipped with their business cards.

- Ideally, they also receive a signed welcome letter from a senior leader in the company.

- All new hires should be assigned a mentor. This could be a colleague, but the most enlightened companies are investing in external professional mentors who are able to mentor and coach the new person through their first 12 months, possibly at regular two-month intervals. This can be done via phone or video call. HPTs generally welcome this type of opportunity, as it assists their desire for growth and success.

By this stage you have put in an immense amount of work finding your new hire, to summarize the key points in this chapter you should remember :

- When identifying the candidate you wish to make an offer to, use all the information you have gathered throughout the process and not just your findings from the final stage. This is particularly important if you are struggling to make a decision or have two candidates you are choosing between.

- When making an offer to the candidate put yourself in their shoes. Are you confident they are going to accept the offer you present to them?

- Continually identify any risks during and after the interview process that may result in you loosing your preferred candidate. Consider what steps can be taken to mitigate them.

- A company induction and engaging on boarding process is essential to the success of a new hire and longevity in the role.

Chapter 9
Staff Retention

However good your hiring strategy is, you should also be looking at how it integrates with staff retention, that is, how well or otherwise you are doing with respect to keeping the organization's staff. This is particularly so if you have focused on securing high performers. If as mentioned in the section on company branding, their EVP is not met they will be leaving pretty quickly. One significant element of change in the employment market place in the last decade is the regularity with which employees are approached by people trying to tempt them away from their current employer. Many people we have spoken to get approached through LinkedIn on an almost daily basis. There used to be a time when it was a flattering thing to be approached. Now everybody can claim to be "headhunted"! It is therefore now more important than ever that employers know how to retain their staff. If not someone will catch them on the wrong day for you, and the first you will know of it is a resignation letter.

Some companies find themselves perplexed over why their employees leave. Some may not care, but this is foolish. If you are one of the companies that is sensible enough to care, then the good news is that there are a number of ways you can look to reduce your staff turnover; but first of all, you need to know what's actually going on – why is this happening?

Employee turnover

The calculation below can be used to work out your staff turnover, which you can use to pick up any trends that may enlighten you as to why you may be failing to retain your employees.

Total number of leavers in a year

Average number of employees in a year   x 100

The average employee turnover rate is in the region of 15% per year. For the legal sector you can expect it to be lower than this this at around 11-12%, if we take a look at Muldowney Legal as an example, they have

> "an attrition rate for losing staff of all types that is double the average for other law firms in Dublin. They have gained an unfortunate reputation as a result"

Let's calculate their current staff turnover rate:

Jan 2019 employed 603 people
During the year they hired 24 new employees and 112 employees left. At the end of the year there was 515 employees.

To work out the average annual staff employed, add the amount of employees at the start of the year (603) to the amount at the end of the year (515) and divide by 2 to get average number employees for the year.

603 + 515 = 1118 / 2 = 559 average number of staff at the end of the year.

Now to calculate the employee turnover as a percentage:

$$\frac{112 \text{ (number of leavers)}}{559 \text{ (average staff)}} \quad 0.20 \times 100 = 20\%$$

Think about it like this from a statistical point of view; if your staff turnover percentage is 20% that means that in 5 years' time the equivalent to the entire population of the firm has effectively been "turned over".

Alongside this they have just recently completed a merger with Knight Murphy Kett LLP and this in itself will see a number of employees leaving through choice or redundancy. We will come to this later.

20% is too high compared to industry norms, very costly, very time consuming and could have a damaging long lasting effect on your employer brand and to the employees that remain. There are, though, a number of things that can be done to change the ever-changing faces of your workforce. It is time to start digging and getting some facts that drive this statistic.

What is the tenure of staff who are leaving?

This is important for a couple of reasons; if employees are leaving within the first 12 months of starting their new job then something has clearly gone wrong. They are the short tenures we refer to earlier. Has their EVP not been met? Did they not get along with their line manager? Was there an issue with team dynamics? Maybe the culture wasn't to their liking?

Anyone that has been with the company for 3 – 5 years it may be just their time to move on and develop their career. It is just as equally important to find this out. Do you consider them to be a high performer and have you missed an opportunity to promote as you were not providing that employee with opportunities to grow and develop?

There are so many reasons why someone may leave a job and it is wise to analyze carefully and split them into categories so you can see exactly where the biggest problems lie. Muldowney may find that their biggest problem is with associate lawyers who are burning out within a particular division within the company because of the long hours they are expected to work. Or it could be that the type of position is not relevant to their decision and that most people are leaving as they do not like the culture of the company, they have grown so quickly in recent years they have lost their identity and as such now don't have one.

Benefits of an exit interview

All this information can be obtained through an exit interview with the employee either face to face or by asking them to complete a form. Sometimes the latter is better as you will find people will be more honest if they can write down exactly how they feel rather than try to explain directly to someone. If you are not sure test it out, but if the problem lies with the same person who is conducting the exit interview, then there is a problem within a problem. On the flip side person to person contact allows you to discuss the concerns raised and allow you to leave a better lasting impression of the company with that person.

High turnover of staff can have both a negative and sometimes even, a positive effect on your business. We will firstly look at the negative impact as a result of high rates of employee attrition in your company:

Overall business performance

Many of Muldowney's clients have been with them for a long time. They have a certain level of expectation in regard to customer care, have got used to dealing with the same people who they feel they know and like and that employees understand their account, their needs, and how to work with them. Imagine you are that client and you ring up as you have always done to speak to the trusted team in employment law and the team who you have worked with for the past few years are no longer there and they have been replaced with new people who are friendly enough but there is no rapport; you are not confident in their knowledge of your account and the service you once enjoyed you feel has gone. When your good employees leave the company and are replaced (in the eyes of the client) by a less experienced worker until that person is trained up, the quality of business and the level of service to your clients will decrease. It is inevitable that situations like this are going to affect your clients, they are going to start questioning how good the service really is and why your staff are leaving. This can then in turn affect your company performance. Some clients may take their business elsewhere which is going to alter your profit margins, company reputation and quality of service.

Of course some employee turnover is inevitable, but it's an issue you want to address proactively. Don't wait for the client to ring up to find out for themselves they are being looked after by someone new, get in touch and reassure them that it is business as usual. The effects of high employee turnover are real, costly and potentially debilitating. These effects can be the polar opposite of what it takes to get supercharged growth!

Distribution of workload and productivity

When people move on from a company, where possible handovers should take place between old employees and new. However, even in these circumstances it is not always possible to handover every single piece of work or every detail on processes and systems and it is never going to be possible to effectively pass on many years of experience in a role. When many employees leave in quick succession the quality and quantity of work output suffers. Some people are learning on the job, so productivity slows down; some information doesn't get passed on so has to be unpicked. If there is no clear management structure or defined responsibilities, then the quality of the work is going to be affected. It is therefore vital that as much information as possible is detailed on how a job role is carried out and what responsibilities fall within it. Be mindful if you are losing a manager and several employees within one division, identify who is the best person to step in as an interim to keep the department running whilst recruitment takes place.

Employer brand and company image

A high attrition rate can damage your company reputation and negative PR can make the difference between a potential employee wanting to work for you or not. The internet and social media are great sources of information and although you should not believe everything that you read there are well regarded websites such as Glassdoor where employees can give feedback on their experiences working for a company. Any good candidate will carry out research into a company they may want to work for or been offered an interview at and if turnover is high this will set off alarm bells for them. As an employer you must be prepared to be questioned on this and have an extremely solid and thought out response. Do not try to convince high-performance talent with weak reasons why you have seen a lot of staff leave. Be honest and talk about changes made to the company and the reasons why being part of the company now is a positive thing.

Team development

Frequent changes in your team make up can have serious implications on a team's ability to establish rapport among its members. They may never find themselves out of the 'forming' or 'storming' stages of team formation (Tuckman's stages of team formation) as they do not have the opportunity to settle and work out each individual team members role. Adjusting to each other's work habits, understanding likes and dislikes can take some time and if this is continually changing productivity cannot reach its best. If you find yourself in this situation find an opportunity to build your teams rapport with one another. Team building sessions in-house/externally or light touch social events after work can help to bond a team.

Is there ever a good time to have staff turnover?

When we look at Muldowney and the recent merger we can expect during this period to see an increase in staff turnover as they manage the structure of the two businesses coming together.

When events like this happen it is expected that some redundancies will be made as it is likely that some roles will be duplicated for example in IT, HR and administration. The key when reviewing the company needs against the skill set available is not to lose your high performers.

This is a good time to carry out a skills audit of all your staff to assess the impact they are having on the business; are they highly productive; do they fit with the high performance criteria. Are they the type of people that can adapt to change and work with management as you transition the culture.

On completion of a skills audit you will have highlighted your underperformers. If underperformance is a consistent issue that has tried to be addressed through a Personal Development Plan, or close management then it may be time to assess whether such an individual has a future within the organization. This is often a very difficult situation to tackle and many organizations duck the issue, particularly if they already have issues with high staff turnover. The harsh reality is that if someone refuses to take measures to improve their performance they are degrading the overall performance of the team. Like with redundancies after a merger, staff turnover may increase following such an audit, though it should result in new, more highly motivated higher performers coming into the organization if your hiring strategy is correct.

Once the workforce is stabilized a moderate level of staff turnover can have a positive impact for a business, it means fresh ideas and new innovation.

Other types of staff turnover that can have a positive impact is if it happens internally. An existing employee is seconded to a different department or permanently relocated to a new team. This is an extremely effective way of retaining your high performers, upskilling your current workforce and developing company culture.

Staff turnover is low but it's the high performers who are leaving

If you don't have high turnover but are losing your best people something isn't working for them and it is your responsibility to find out what that is and try to uncover this before you are handed the next letter of resignation. Regular 1:1s with line management is essential, but not just for a chatty catch up. They need to be productive, action based and challenging in a positive way. How is the individual working towards their objectives, are these challenging enough? Where are the opportunities for training and development? High performers require a career plan and goals. They will be highly effective in the job by their very nature but after a period of time they will start to ask what next and if you are not able to offer them opportunities, they may look elsewhere. The benefits of hiring and retaining a high performer vastly outweigh the negatives as highlighted throughout the book.

Let's look at the positive side of staff turnover, when it is kept within an acceptable and manageable level:

How to work with staff turnover to develop a high performance workforce

A certain level of low staff turnover is most likely healthy for your business. If you have persistent underperformers who are missing their performance objectives on a regular basis with no mitigating personal circumstances then you may decide to have a company policy that states if an employee is not achieving at a certain level of minimum performance then they should be replaced. Your replacement method should be to recruit high performers. While we do not necessarily endorse such a strategy, companies such as Netflix and General Electric (GE) have been said to employ a bottom 10% rule. If you are in the bottom 10% then you will be replaced! If your company opts for such a strategy you will need to decide what exceptions there might be. Too ruthless a strategy in this area might be counter-productive to your employer brand, but equally to allow poor performers to carry on without sanction may be equally damaging to the moral of your hard working and diligent staff members.

To encourage innovations and creation
High performers will have a mindset that means they will strive to be innovative and creative to achieve success. If you have too many people who have become complacent in their job roles or do not have this inner drive your business can become stagnant which not only can have a negative impact on your profitability but on the high performers that you employee. They will get frustrated as they will start to feel that nothing gets done or they are not working with like-minded people, then you run the risk of high performers moving on and being left with those that have poor levels of commitment. Staff turnover may be

legitimately used to create opportunity to employee innovators and idea generators. New additions will have a different perspective to your existing workforce and will energize your high performers. A diverse workforce will help shape the direction of your business and move you to a higher level of skill and performance.

Review your employee appraisal and incentive schemes.
When was the last time you reviewed your employee costs and incentive schemes? As turnover of staff occurs this provides an opportunity to assess your compensation and benefits policies. You may discover that a number of people within the same division have left because your compensation package is below market expectations.

You can carry out an assessment on staff appraisals and evaluate if they are measuring and monitoring performance effectively. Just because that is the way things have always been done does not mean it is the best way for your business right now. Such a review will highlight if your appraisal scheme is picking up underperformers and if the right methods are in place to improve the output before more extreme measures need to be taken. Or if you are potentially losing high performers as your appraisal system is not picking up key areas of development for those individuals.

In the current dynamic employment market your employees must be able to adapt and change, be willing to learn new things and take opportunities to develop. If you have employees that are not open to this you must consider if they are still the right person for your company. High performers are not afraid to give things a try and relish in being given opportunities to try new things. If you have someone who is holding their team back then it may be time to find a different role for that person, and replace them with someone who can bring a new skill set that will keep you in line but better still ahead of the competition.

We have looked at the negative and positive of staff turnover and the impact this can have on your organization and your employees. There are a number of schemes and strategies that can be introduced to any organization that will not only encourage people to work for you but also give your employees a reason to stay.

Staff Retention Strategies

The best overall strategy to retaining your staff is to build a strong culture. A company with a strong positive culture and reputation is harder to leave than one that does not have these attributes. This is in many ways an extension of your employer brand strategy. If you have ever worked for a company where employees genuinely believe that none of their competitors are in the same league, you will understand how powerful this is. Imagine you are playing for a top flight football club and someone suggests that you should play for one in a lower league. Would you consider it? If you are a top performer the answer is probably no. Your company does not have to be a market leader to achieve this. You can achieve it through becoming a market leading employer, even if you are not the biggest name in your sector. Many start-ups achieve this through providing outstandingly "cool" workplaces. If you love where you work, why are you going to listen to an approach from a company that doesn't have a similar reputation or ethos ?

Companies that achieve such employer brand leadership status normally have a number of things in common. A fundamental is their management capability that runs right the way through the organization with consistency. This is rarely achieved without excellent management training and a values led approach from the top. Such a structure communicates clearly, it makes people feel strongly appreciated and provides opportunities for personal growth and innovation. One of the most common reasons for someone leaving a job is because of poor management. What is less well appreciated is the number of times individuals decline a new opportunity because of loyalty to a manager, team or brand.

A high quality individual who is exceptional in their own field should be able to grow their abilities and feel they have an appropriate level of challenge in their work to keep it interesting. Each individual should also be encouraged to come up with ideas on how the culture of the organization can improve and also grow Essentially you should nurture a culture in which individuals feel they are strong stakeholders in that culture and the company's collective mission and success. Your corporate culture should not be static, but should genuinely reflect the people that make up that culture.

Often managers and leaders of companies wrongly assume people mainly leave because they are not paid enough. This can sometimes be the case, but more often it is an additional factor, unless the employer is way below the industry standards. However, some compensation and benefits packages can have significant impact on employee retention.

Bonuses and commissions that are paid at certain times of the year may cause an employee to think twice before making a hasty decision to look at another job offering.

Better still may be Long Term Incentive Plans (LTIP). These are common for senior people, particularly in US Corporations. More forward thinking companies have also extended these to all staff.

Often the best LTIPs are the simplest to understand. Essentially you are looking to reward people who have shown loyalty to the company by remaining for a specified period. The incentive needs to be seen as significant, and perhaps too good to throw away by moving elsewhere. The incentive might be monetary, based on shares, or share options that are given to the employee at preferential rates, and would be worth a considerable sum when vested. Alternatively, it might be an extended paid holiday/vacation allowance that would be difficult to match elsewhere. Some employers offer sabbaticals.

Whatever the offering, it should be designed to improve your retention from where it is today. If you know that your average salesperson leaves after 4 years, at a time when they are often most effective, why not put in place an LTIP that benefits them at 5 or 6 years? You can easily work out the ROI on this. If you offered them a one month sabbatical it might mean you lose them for a month, but that is better than having to rehire for the position, perhaps they will come back reenergized and want to work a further 5 years so they can do it again!

Clearly staff retention is a huge topic and we have barely scratched the surface here (could actually write a whole book about it!). However, this chapter is to highlight that when you hire HPT you should do your best to keep them.

This chapter has:

- Shown why understanding your staff turnover and how implementing strategies to identify reasons for people leaving will help you to avoid future leavers.

- Provided areas for you to review on staff turnover and if these are in fact impacting your own business negatively.

- Shown ways in which staff turnover can have a positive impact on your business and at times used as an advantage.

- Given ideas on implementing staff retention strategies that actually meet the needs of the employees to help you retain your HPT.

Epilogue

What then, will our example companies have learned from their recent recruiting experience had they followed the advice contained in this book:

Muldowney Law are highly fortunate in many respects. They have a forward thinking, progressive HR Director in Megan Doyle. She has introduced structure and process with a key overall objective which is to improve the quality of the people selected to in turn improve performance and retention. The high staff turnover which has been a feature of the last 3 years has now slowed dramatically and performance is now significantly above the average for similar firms. The firm's board have recognized her significant contribution, which in turn has resulted in a number of her own issues being resolved. Her own dissatisfaction with her position has now changed and it is likely she will stay with the firm for many years to come!

The three founders of SGT have been through a very steep learning curve. Their somewhat naïve approach to growing their team started well, but then almost resulted in catastrophic failure to reach their milestones. Fortunately for them the non-executive directors on their board were able to insist on corrective action that resulted in them being able to get their hiring process back on track. Their approach to "candidate generating" is much more aligned to the needs of a fast growing business and their processes are much faster and more efficient. They still have a tendency toward hiring in their own image, but they are being challenged on this and they are seeing the benefits of a more diverse workforce as a result.

Acme Medical has had a highly successful launch of their new product range with their new team in Europe. There has been excellent team work between Lena Rollinger and Tim Brooker, where the hiring of the new team was made a strategic imperative for the broader organization, with a highly structured process that fully integrated Acme staff and their professional partners. They have managed to attain a team that is defined by high performance and professionalism, and the impact that they have already had is immense. The quality of the team has enabled Lena to revise up her projections for sales in the short medium and long term.

The fundamental all three organizations have learned is that you can radically improve your company performance through a strong focus on improving your hiring processes, and the opportunities for companies to use digital strategies to enhance this to outcompete their competitors is immense. They will continue to monitor their progress and look at strategies and tactics that will enable them to be seen as employer of choice for the very best people.

Summary

Successful interviewing, selection and retention is, like most other things in life, a function of a good-quality process. If the recruitment market in general really is broken, there is no necessity for your company to be part of that broken system. In fact, it is an opportunity for you to compete with companies that are using outmoded and inefficient systems, or are attempting to use modern methods but are doing it poorly. If, on the other hand, your process is best in class, you are giving yourself the maximum chance to hire and retain the highest quality employees and supercharge growth.

The opportunities that the internet, and particularly social media, offer savvy job seekers is enormous. No longer are they dependent on being relatively passive in their job searches, as they would have done in the past. Now they can really seek out the very best of employers, or when they are approached they are able to research companies to a level that they would never have been able to before. This in turn offers opportunities to forward thinking companies. Those that really embrace the approaches we have outlined in this book will be putting themselves in the best position to attract these high performers and high potentials. The social media age enables companies of all sizes and types to compete for the very best people.

These steps and suggestions should form part of a strategy and though they cannot not guarantee success with every hire, they will help you work out a system that ensures that your organization is following the very best practice, thereby giving you the maximum chance of hiring and retaining genuine High Performance Talent.

These people will be the powerhouses behind High Performance Companies that are rapidly growing in the digital age . Is recruitment broken? Not for the companies and individuals that know how to use the latest methods.

ABOUT THE AUTHORS

Nigel Job

After an initial career in technical sales and marketing in the field of healthcare, Nigel set up an executive recruitment company, Remtec Search and Selection, in 1998 (now known as Remtec Talent Management). Since then he has established a system for evaluating and attracting high performers for clients, which has been based on the study, observation and measurement of a wide range of individuals from all parts of the world.

Lorna Rutter

Having worked in the executive recruitment and talent acquisition sector since 2006 alongside Nigel Job, Lorna has worked on hiring systems and processes that over time have aided companies to attract the very best talent and equally find the very best talent their perfect jobs. Lorna is a firm believer in making sure those systems and processes are tailored to meet the needs of the individual client and applicant. This book enables companies to define and refine their currents processes and procedures to ensure they achieve the ultimate outcomes.

Influences on the thinking behind "Is Recruitment Broken", and further reading.

- The 7 Habits of Highly effective People, Stephen Covey

- Sales EQ, Jeb Blount

- In Search of Excellence Lessons from America's Best-Run Companies, Tom Peters and Robert Waterman

- Employer Brand Management: Practical Lessons from the World's Leading Employers, Richard Mosley

- The Vibrant Workplace: Overcoming the Obstacles to Building a Culture of Appreciation, Paul White

- Discover Your True North, Bill George

- Hiring For Attitude, Mark Murphy

- The Essential Guide for Hiring & Getting Hired: Performance-based Hiring Series. Lou Adler

- Resilience: Facing Down Rejection and Criticism on the Road to Success, Mark McGuinness

- Originals: How Non-Conformists Move the World, Adam Grant

- Think and Grow Rich, Napoleon Hill

- Warren Buffett: a Biography, Daniel Jones

- The Motivation Myth. How High Achievers Really Set Themselves Up to Win, Jeff Haden

- Competitiveness Reconceptualized: Psychometric Development of the Competitiveness Orientation Measure as a Unified Measure of Trait Competitiveness, Jennifer L. Newby & Rupert G. Klein, The Psychological Record Vol 64 Issue 4 pp 879–895

DISCLAIMER

While efforts have been made by the authors to verify the ideas and information in this publication neither they nor the publisher assumes any responsibility for any omissions or errors or interpretations of the subject matter. The views and ideas contained in this book do not in any way constitute commands or instructions and the reader is responsible for their actions and interpretation. The advice may not be suitable for all individuals and businesses and the author shall not be liable for any damages arising from any attempts to follow the examples or exercises herein. Adherence to all applicable laws and regulations covering professional conduct, business practices, recruitment and all other aspects of doing business in any jurisdiction in the world is the sole responsibility of the purchaser or reader. If in any doubt, the reader is advised to consult appropriate professional advisors in the geographical area that they conduct business.

END

Printed in Great Britain
by Amazon